Between us

Ruby Dhal

Ruby Dhal

Written and arranged by Ruby Dhal

Piction Books Ltd

Other books by Ruby

About This Book

This book is a bridge between the old and new. Between who I was and who I have become. Hence the title *'Between us'*.

This book is a true journey of love, growth, and life. Several pieces in this book were written by 21-year-old me but never shared or published. I was trying to find my identity and understand myself as a writer and I tended to dabble with different styles of writing, all of which have been shared in this special bundle of healing. But there are also pages and pages of writing by 26-year-old me. The me who had published 4 books of poetry, prose and self-help and looked like she had everything figured out —but she continued to get hurt, learn, and heal all over again. The me that decided to write some more to find the strength so she could walk on the journey of life. The me who writes as though she has all the wisdom of the world, but she still makes mistakes and learns from them. Because I'm only human. Because there is only so much energy I can put into saving my relationships. Because the previous year-and-a-half has been hard. So hard.

So incredibly hard.

I can't begin to explain the kaleidoscopic journey of emotions that I have surged through this previous year. The love I have felt and shared. The people I have lost. The memories I have let slip between my fingers like particles of sand into an ocean of nostalgic longing. Love has poured out of me into the hearts of all those I care about, but I have lost, *oh, how I have lost*. And that loss is something that I am going to take forward with me for years to follow. That loss is going to squeeze itself into a tight corner of my heart, for fear that if it comes to the fore —then it might obliterate all the happiness that envelopes the rest of my life. The experiential difference between the 21-year-old-me and the 26-year-old-me equates to a stylistic difference as well. This means that *'Between us'* is my most unique book, where the old meshes with the new and who I was meets who I have become to make something beautiful. Where Ruby-then and Ruby-now share their stories and pour their heart into pages and pages of this book. And maybe you will realise it too. Maybe you will be able to tell the difference between Ruby-then and Ruby-now. Maybe you will be able to appreciate the hurt I felt before and the woman I have become. Maybe you will notice how soft my heart was and how much stronger it has since gotten, but maybe you will still find a link between those two.

But if you do —promise me that you will keep it *between us…*

Love,

Ruby Dhal x

"She decided long ago that life was a long journey. She would be strong, and she would be weak, and both would be okay."

—*Furthermore, by* Tahereh Mafi

Oh, but you are so strong in all your softness.

Life doesn't go according to plan.

But isn't that the beauty of it? Because somehow, somewhere, everything always manages to fall into place.

Never let yourself feel low because of the way another person treats you. You need to understand that you are worth so much more than what that person has to offer, and one day someone will appreciate you and treat you right. But even if they don't, even if you don't find someone else who is able to see all the magic that resides within you —you can find that magic within yourself and give your heart all the love that it deserves.

The truth is we never really forget people. We might forget the minute detail of our conversations, the banter that we shared on social media or what their dog's name was —but we never truly *forget them*. We don't forget what made them smile, or the name of the book that made them come alive. We don't forget the song that they would sing at the top of their lungs in the car or their favourite flavour of gelato from that place in the city. We don't forget the tears we shed together or the deep night-time conversations we shared. We don't forget every time they lent us their shoulder to cry on or the arguments we tossed back and forth. We don't forget the adventures, the laughter or the smiles. We don't forget the pain they caused and what pushed us away either. We don't forget the hurting, the learning and the growth. The truth is, we never really forget people. We just get really good at pretending that they never happened. We tell ourselves that we don't remember what it was like because it makes it easier to live life without them.

Preferences

And you know what doesn't make sense? How you want things so badly at one point in your life that you would do anything for them. Like a job. A relationship. His love. Her attention. A holiday. A family. Something that you think will fulfil you at that particular point, but when you finally get it —you don't want it anymore. I just don't understand how it's possible for you to want love from someone so desperately at one point in your life that it's all you ever think about. And when you finally receive it, when they are finally declaring their love to you —you realise that it's not what you want anymore. I don't understand how we, as humans, change our preferences and have constantly altering feelings towards people, things and places all the time. Because, then what is real? What is stable? When will you ever know whether you genuinely want someone or just want them because you think that you can't have them, but when you get them —you decide that you don't want them anymore? When will our feelings be real and our wishes true? And the more serious question is —will they ever be real? Will we ever know that we want something and stick to it? And you know what I don't understand most of all; how we can be so in love with someone at a point in our lives but at another point —not feel a thing. That just doesn't make sense to me.

The one thing that I have learnt from this whole experience is that I have spent years taking life for granted. I used to put off meeting family and friends on the assumption that I would see them again. I would make excuses. *I've had a long day at work and I'm too tired to meet up. I just want to stay at home today and relax. I can't meet next week because I've got so many plans. I'll call you back in 10 minutes.* But I would never make that call. Either I would forget, or I would get busy doing other things, or I would put it off for later. Later. As though it is confirmed that there will be another occasion, another opportunity to meet, another chance. I thought that I had all the time in the world and so did my family and friends and everyone else that I care about. But life is so short and our time limited.

As much as I want to say that I will make all the plans and come out every time after this is all over, I don't want to make promises that I can't keep. But what I can promise is this —I will try harder. I will make more effort to check up on those that I care about. I will listen attentively. I will apologise profusely for being so caught up in my own life and my own problems. I will make the calls that I said I would, and I will show my care more than I have in the past. I will be there. I will show up.

And I will not take anyone that I love for granted ever again.

—my time with covid-19

Tell me what to think when there is an empty space
in my heart where you once belonged. Does it mean
that I finally moved on or does it mean that you did?

What does it mean to love yourself?

Let me tell you what it doesn't mean. It doesn't mean being selfish, aggressive, egotistical and prioritising your needs over other people's, time and time again. It doesn't mean spending all your money on clothes and gadgets or spending all your energy on pampering others. Unless clothes and gadgets make you happy —then do what you must to furnish that happiness. But remember —you will never find true happiness in contingent things. You will always want the next gadget, the next item of clothing, the next *'high'* until you admit that your happiness and the love that you give yourself must come from deep within. It also doesn't mean doing everything for others and nothing for yourself. It doesn't mean giving yourself the bare minimum while giving others everything that you have got. It doesn't mean accepting less than what you deserve, just because you don't want to hurt them.

Loving yourself means saying *'yes'* to selfcare, to putting yourself first —but not at the expense of others— to pampering yourself, to listening to your heart and to learning more about what you need. Loving yourself means making a list of goals and dreams that will furnish your life, to doing things that bring you joy. Loving yourself means understanding yourself better. Loving yourself doesn't mean hurting others at the cost of your own happiness, and it doesn't mean hurting yourself at the cost of theirs. Loving yourself means taking into consideration what other people need but also focusing on what you deserve. Loving yourself is a balance of caring about your wellbeing but also considering other people's feelings and abiding by your responsibility towards them.

There is beauty in vulnerability. There is strength in accepting your weaknesses. There is power in pointing out your blemishes and scars. There is grace in voicing your imperfections. There is so much within you to offer yourself and others —and it would be messy to think that your tiny *'darkness'* has the power to dim your light. If anything —all it does is make you burn brighter.

5 things I learned about love/dating in my 20s:

1. You will constantly pick the *'wrong'* people if you don't let your version of love grow with you.

2. Never listen to those who tell you to *'settle'* for someone before you run out of time because what you want *does not exist* —all the core traits that you are searching for in a partner are real and will manifest if you are patient enough to find them.

3. There is no *'right person'* —someone is only right for you if they are healthy for your heart and for your mind.

4. Don't fall for potential. Fall for actions. If someone acts like they don't care about you —the odds are that this is true. Accept this and move on.

5. Love changes over time —both within a relationship and between relationships. This means that maybe you have not stopped loving each other, instead, you both need to reconcile your meaning of love with the growth of your relationship.

Sometimes all you really want is for someone to understand how you're feeling. But it's so hard to express your exact emotions. I mean, how can you when you're barely able to put them in words? How can you when you don't know what to make of everything that you've experienced? But still —you want another person to listen to the words that flutter through the beating of your heart and say, *'I know how you feel and I'm here for you'*. Still, you want someone to be there for you as you try to figure out the mess that has been made of your life. Still, you wish someone were by your side —with love breathing through their lungs for you— as you tread through the trenches of your ache. Still, you want someone to *try to understand* how you are feeling, even if you can't put it in words. Still, you wish you had someone's shoulder to lay your head on and their hand to hold. Just this once. Just this once.

Comparison

Comparison is the biggest threat to happiness. Comparing your outfit, physical appearance, education, career, relationships, and love-life to others can have the worst effect on your life. Because you think that other people's highlights are what your every day should look like. And that is wrong. Turning to other people's lives to idealise your own *'perfect'* existence not only sets unrealistic standards for all areas of your life —but it results in immense disappointment when your life doesn't turn out in that *'picture-perfect'* way you thought it would. Remember the phrase, *'The grass is greener where you water it'*, and nothing could be more honest than this —because your life will be as beautiful as your actions show. If you make effort in cultivating healthy relationships, then your relationships will blossom. If you work hard towards your goals and dreams, then they will eventually show the fruition of all the hours that you put in. If you wake up each morning with a grateful mindset then life will correspond to that bright picture, rather than represent the dim reality that you falsely believe it is when you look at other people's highlight reels.

But this doesn't mean that your life won't have difficulties. Manifesting a good life and *'watering'* the grass of your relationships, career and growth does not mean that sometimes you won't fail, have problems or get your heart broken. Because, sure, the sun rises every day, but it does not always shine. Because that is what life is about —struggles, pain, learning and growth and, following that, happiness, love, peace. Life is not one shade of perfect. It is a kaleidoscope of pain, change, and love. And I know you think that your pain is worse than others, that your struggles are heavier, just because other people look like they are having the best time. But that's not true. No one shares their unhappiness on social media. People don't post about their bad days and if they do then they have gathered enough strength to be able to do so. And you should gather the same amount of strength to know that no two souls are the same so how could two lives be? No two people are the same so how could their happiness be compared? It can't be. It just can't.

The day you understand that comparison does nothing good for your life and does more to diminish your happiness is the day you will deeply appreciate your entire life —including the good and bad— and know, with certainty that your life is as *'perfect'* as could be.

Be kind to others. Be delicate with their heart. Don't take their emotions lightly. We don't know what other people are going through —and the least we can do is make their journey softer.

Phenomenon

Love is a weird phenomenon. You look at one person and suddenly your heart decides that your whole universe will revolve around them. You tie your emotions, your happiness, your wishes and your dreams to that one human as if they have all the answers to every question about your life. Love is so weird because —if you think about it— it is completely irrational to hold one person as the centre of your existence. It is completely irrational to think that just their presence is enough to make everything okay. Just one smile on their face is enough to make our day. Just one hug has the power to solve all our problems. It is completely irrational.

But still, we do it anyway. We fall for people, and we let them fall for us in the most beautiful way possible, as if that is what destiny requires from us. Love is so unimaginably magnificent that despite it all, despite its irrationality, despite its ability to control everything in our lives and despite the undeniable pain it brings with it, I don't think we would have it any other way.

Women create women. Women empower women. Women guide women. Women hold women together with love, with integrity, with kindness. Women support women. But women do not break women.

I repeat —women do not break women.

Losing people is never going to be easy. No matter how much other people tell you that time will heal your heart or that the years will ease your pain. Sometimes they just won't. Sometimes, the loss is so great that no matter how much time passes and how many years trail by since they left your side —the emptiness will always be there. It will always hurt. And that will always be the case when someone you love passes. Because how can you stop missing them? How can you tell yourself that the time you had with them was enough? It will never be enough. It cannot be. You will always wish for another day. Another hour. Another moment to have spent with them so you could tell them how much they mean to you. To hug them. To see their smiling face for the last time. To remind them —that no matter what happens— you will always love them. You will always miss them. You will always feel their absence like a hard rock inside your chest and nothing can ever change that.

Sometimes loss is loss and there is nothing more to it other than a pain so deep that it walks with you forever. Because that is how much it hurts when people are gone forever. That is how much it hurts when someone you love passes away.

—I will always love you, uncle
Rest in peace, 22/02/2021

I guess that is the issue with feeling everything so deeply
—sometimes I say too little and sometimes

I say too much.

Not everyone is going to be kind to you. Not everyone will be gentle to your heart or make an attempt to understand your journey. And sometimes it just won't make sense. It won't make sense why this person is being rude *'for no reason'* or has acted against your welfare, when you wouldn't do that to them. Sometimes it doesn't make sense why others are mean or harsh or *'play games'* with your life and theirs. Because we are not built that way. We don't see life in the way that they do. We don't know what they've witnessed or experienced that has made them this way, but the one truth we know is this —nothing justifies it. Nothing justifies them treating people badly on purpose. Nothing justifies them hurting us. Nothing justifies them being selfish or inconsiderate. And even if we can't change them, we can still change ourselves around them —especially if we can't avoid them. We can teach ourselves to stay out of their way or adopt tiny behaviours that will help us deal with these people. Because the truth is that not everyone is going to be nice to you —and instead of trying and failing to change them, we have to gather strength and change ourselves so we can deal with it in a way that is good for us.

Your partner isn't here to fix you and a relationship is not the cure to all your problems. The amount of people that believe a relationship will be the key to living a happy life is unbelievable. This leads to broken people getting into relationships that they weren't ready for with the hope that their brokenness will be fixed. And when that doesn't happen and they realise that they still have a void in their life —they either get into more relationships to continue to fill that void or they come out of their current relationship even more broken, even more unhappy than before. The key to living a happy life isn't to find someone who will fill your emptiness —but to find ways to fill it all by yourself.

Stay

I can't do it anymore. This pretending. This telling myself that I don't care, or at least —I shouldn't care. Because how can I not? How can I not care about someone that I loved as my own? How can I tell myself that leaving you behind is okay because it's the right thing to do? How could something that is supposed to be right feel so wrong? It doesn't make sense. It just doesn't. And all I want to do is text you to see if you are okay All I want to do is give you a ring to see if you want to meet up for a catch-up over coffee or brunch, just so I can see your smiling face. Just so I can hug you, hold you or sit by your side. Just like old times. Love is so difficult when the person you love is no longer in your life. It's just so damn hard to tell yourself that it's okay to move on in your life. That it's okay to say goodbye. It's okay to never turn back and look at them. It's okay to think that this was for the best. Because it doesn't feel like it. It doesn't feel like any of this will be okay, and that is the hardest of all —telling my heart that it's okay to let you go when all I want to do is make you stay.

Things to stop doing this year:

1. Making excuses for other people.

2. Refusing to listen to your heart.

3. Having self-doubt.

4. Not following your dreams.

5. Believing that you are not enough
   (for that job, that goal or that relationship).

6. Not acknowledging your achievements;
   both big and small.

7. Stepping down when you need to
   stand up for yourself.

8. Doing things that you dislike.

Hold On

Sometimes we tell ourselves that it's hard to let someone go, but it's not as hard as we think —we just choose not to cut them off. You see, we are so attached to this person and we are so used to having them in our life that the idea of them not being there doesn't sit well with us. Even if they cause us pain, we choose to have them in our lives, even if they become toxic to our hearts, we hold on to all the instances when they were not bad for us, and we use that as an excuse not to leave them. It is self-destructive, this constant justificatory cycle that we find ourselves in —making excuses for their actions, just because leaving them would cause us pain, rather than focusing on the fact that having them in our lives isn't any better. Yes, they make us happy. Yes, they bring sunshine in our lives. But if the pain they cause us is just as much —then we must let them go. I agree that there must be a balance of light and dark, but that balance does not need to come from just *one person.* We must keep only those in our lives who give love us and without whom life would not be the beautiful journey that it is.

Sometimes we hold on to people who hurt us because letting go of them would hurt us even more. Sometimes we let the people we love break us because they make us feel complete. And that doesn't make sense. We hold on to the darkness they give us because they bring us light. We hold on to the pain because they make us happy, and we keep holding on to them even though —deep down— we know that we should let them go. Sometimes we hold on to people who hurt us just because they make us happy, and that is what doesn't make sense about us.

Blessings

Some people are absolute blessings. They are the kind of people who make you wish upon shooting stars. The kind of people that make you smile even when they are not around as just one thought of them is enough to brighten your day. They are pure souls. Souls that don't know how to hurt others or be selfish. Souls that only wish to spread goodness, light and positivity wherever they go. Souls that are innocent, genuine and so detached from the mundane world with its imperfections that you almost want to be like them. They are too good to be true. Magical almost. But believe me —such people exist. And when you come across someone like that, the only thing you find yourself asking is *'Where have you been my whole life?'*, and that is when you know you have found someone absolutely amazing. Someone who is a blessing in disguise.

Love Yourself

Love yourself enough to let them go. Enough to say *'no'* when they are asking for too much. Enough to stick up for yourself. Enough to demand your right. Enough to assert it. Enough to stop giving and giving without asking for anything in return. Love yourself enough to put yourself first. Enough to stop letting people walk all over you. Enough to say what you feel —with your head held high and your shoulders spread wide. With no fear for what they will think —because you have nothing to shy away from. Love yourself enough to accept your truths. Your shortcomings. Your scars. Enough to embrace your imperfections and to find strength in all your vulnerabilities. Love yourself enough to wait for the love you deserve. Enough to remove any thoughts of *'settling'* on your mind. Enough to understand that the love that you are worth —you will receive. Enough to accept the truth that it hasn't worked out with anyone because they were not meant for you. Enough to know, with certainty, that someone will come along and teach you how to spill self-love into all your cracks. One day someone will come along and show you how whole you were, and how much you don't need them or anyone else to be happy, and how invaluable you are. How imperfectly perfect you are.

Love yourself enough to walk away. Please, do it for you. Love yourself enough to walk away.

Fear holds you back. It wraps itself around your ankles and stops you from moving forward, especially when you cross a pedestal with someone emotionally. Fear of getting your heart broken. Fear of falling too quickly. Fear of loving too much. Fear of loving too little. Fear of not being capable to love. Fear of giving too much of yourself away. Fear of not being strong enough to commit. Fear of making a mistake. Fear of never being enough. Fear of them not being the one. Fear is what holds us all back. Fear is what stops us from loving at all.

Validation

It is difficult to tell yourself that other people can't validate you when you spend most of your life looking to them for the answers that you're not able to find. How does one change their entire way of living in a second? They can't. It takes time. It takes time to accept that other people can't affirm your existence or worth because you've spent so long making them —and yourself— believe that they can. That they have the power to decide whether that outfit looks good on you, whether your job is good and whether your relationship is worthy of you. You have spent so long giving these people the remote to your self-esteem, that when you finally realise how wrong you were to rely on them for all the important opinions that you should have formed yourself —you come to terms with how difficult it will now be to de-tangle your relationship with them from this role that you've given them. And the only way to do this without hurting them is to form healthy boundaries. Boundaries which allow you to kindly inform others that you respect their opinion —but it will not guide you in making your decision.

And this will be hard to accept at first —for both you and them. Because when you are so used to relying on other people for comforting advice that makes your life easier, and when they are so used to giving it to you, it becomes difficult to not only set new boundaries but to live up to them. But this is something you must do if you want to engage in healthy relationships with those that love and care about you. This is something you must do if you want to start affirming yourself, while respecting that other people will always have something to say —but instead of giving their opinions the power to control your life, knowing that you have *the power to choose* whether you want to take their opinions on board when making your decisions.

It can be very comforting to depend on those you care about to guide the direction of your journey —but if they aren't living your life, then they won't be able to talk meaningfully about it. And this is something you need to embrace if you want to start taking control of how your journey looks, rather than letting others decide for you.

I once said to a friend, 'I don't understand what pushes people to be awful. I just don't get it'. And my friend looked at me over her glasses, her eyes planted on my weary face, a frown formed across her forehead, her lips a thin red line. 'It's because they don't have the same heart as you,' she said.

'You will never know how much darkness others hold in their heart because your own heart is filled with so much light. You will never figure out why they treat you badly, say harsh words or sabotage their relationships because your heart doesn't work that way. It never has. And I know it doesn't make sense. It doesn't make sense why people want the worst for those who would never wish the same upon them —but you are not in their shoes. You don't know what kind of battles they faced that have turned them so stone-hearted that no amount of love can melt them back to softness. But this doesn't mean that they are excused for the hurt they cause. It just means that you need to stop trying so hard to understand them so you can justify their behaviour. Because other people don't have the same heart as you, and no matter how much you tell yourself that maybe one day they will change — maybe they won't. Because being like this helps them walk through life better somehow, because there's a reason why they have become this way.'

We don't really fall in love with people.

We fall in love with *souls* mirrored through eyes.

Find yourself the kind of person who shows you that the most beautiful people are effortlessly imperfect. The kind of person who doesn't try to hide their weaknesses, their fears or their blemishes. The kind of person who accepts themselves the way you wish you could. Find yourself the kind of person who makes you fall in love with the possibility of imperfection within someone who seems so perfect. Find yourself a perfectly imperfect person, and you will never be scared to fall in love again.

Okay Again

I need you to know that you will get through this. I need you to have faith in yourself and the plan bigger than you and all of us and keep on going. I need you to stop believing what other people say, or do, or feel about your situation. Because they are not you. They haven't had a taste of your life, breathed through your experiences or seen the world through your weathered-red eyes. They don't know what you need —but you do. You need to believe that this day, and the next, and the one after that is preparing you for strength, for growth, and for a love so undeniably real that it could drown you, but it won't. I need you to keep going. I need you to swallow the pain as you would medicine and drink self-love in the way you would drink water to wash away the bitter after-taste. Because it won't taste bitter for too long, trust me. I need you to let time work its healing power by accepting the changes that come your way, by accepting new people, experiences and foreign emotions. Because time can only work if you let it, so you must let it if you want to heal. You must let it if you want to feel happiness. You must let it if you want to move on. And you must let it if you want to feel okay again.

What You Deserve

You deserve happiness. You deserve to wake up with the love of your life by your side on a lazy Sunday morning as the sun casts a yellow light over your face. You deserve to catch up with friends over coffee and brunch and share memories and laughter, feeling more alive than you have felt in the longest time. You deserve to plop a kiss on your mum's forehead and cuddle your dad as his soft fluffy sweater sweeps against your cheek. You deserve adventures and days out, as well as cosy days in with the people that you care about the most. You deserve to tell the people you love that you love them, and you deserve to tell them when you need space too. You deserve to spend time alone, even if it means doing nothing other than watching TV or listening to the radio as you have some *'me time'*. You deserve a warm long bath, and you deserve a cold, wintry walk through the park. Because, my love, you deserve everything that you told yourself you didn't deserve and so, so much more.

To everyone that I have hurt on my healing journey:

I am sorry for causing you the kind of pain that I can't undo even if I tried. I was just trying to find my way, but I am so sorry that you lost yours in the process.

Differences between the right vs. the wrong person:

The right person will make effort with you. If they care about you and want to know you more then they will try their best to put time and energy into making this work. The wrong person will not invest as much time/effort into you. They will speak to you when it's convenient for them, they won't pick up the phone as much and they will not invest their energy into getting to know you.

The right person will make their intentions clear to you. If they like you then they will tell you. Words like *'relationship', 'dating'* and *'commitment'* won't scare them and they will be vocal in their appreciation of you. The wrong person will play games. They will insinuate that they like you and openly flirt but when you will confront them, they will either deny this or label you as a *'friend',* a *'buddy'* or a *'best friend'.*

The right person will want to meet you. If they are sure that they like you then they will plan dates and clear their calendar to spend time with you. The wrong person will either want to meet you straight away without knowing you —in which case, they have other reasons— or they will make excuses when you suggest meeting them. They might even meet you once to tick it off just so you don't mention it again.

Best Time of Your Life

I've spent my entire life losing people, and I've reached a point where I wonder whether I will ever feel like myself again. I don't know how to explain it all. The gap between the pieces of my heart. The jitteriness in my stomach when I remember that I can never go back to some of the most incredible moments of my life. The emptiness. The silence. The relationships that have left a hole inside my soul but filled my mind with so many memories that I don't know what to do with them. That I don't know how to make sense of it all.

Isn't it weird? You can have the most amazing moments ever without knowing it, without being aware that this time will go down in history as your happiest. But when it passes you by like particles of sand slipping through your fingers —you're left with a pining ache at the pit of your heart for a time long gone. Because that is how it feels —losing people. Losing experiences and moments. *Losing time.* Because once those people are gone, those moments feel like a dream that you won't have the chance to visit again. And it is so hard. It is so damn hard telling yourself that everything happened for the best —because now you're sitting on the side-line, watching the movie of your life play before you and wondering whether you will ever get to re-live the best parts again. Wondering whether you will ever experience those incredible joys with the people you love and know —*in that moment*— that this is the best time of your life.

Sometimes, the pain doesn't go away. It just doesn't. Because how could it? How could losing someone close to you stop hurting? How could it not feel like you didn't lose a huge part of your soul when they passed? It's not easy. It will never be easy. Because every time you look at a photo of them —all you see are memories of a time that has long passed you by. And no matter how much you wish you could change your present, no matter how much you wish you could bring them back —you can't. And that is what hurts the most. You can't change that second when your life changed forever. You can't turn back time. You can't go back to the last moment you spent together to tell them that you love them. That you will never stop loving them. That —no matter what happens— their memories will be the glue that holds all your pieces together. And their absence will never leave you. You will learn to live with it. You will learn to accept it. But you will never be able to move on. Because you can't. You just can't. Because sometimes the pain does not go away. And rather than learning how to move on from the loss —you have to learn how to move forward with it.

Meant for You

Maybe this is how it was meant to be. Maybe you were meant to break your heart on the hands of someone you loved because you needed to be shown what love was. Maybe you both parted ways because staying in each other's lives any longer would have caused you more pain than leaving would. And that is why they left. Or you did. And that's why things ended so horribly that now even thinking about what was brings a stone lump to your throat that you try and try to swallow down but can't. But it is okay. Not the pain or the anguish. But the journey. It's okay to feel like this because there is no other way to feel. There is no other way to remember those moments without pining for them. Without missing them. Without hurting for them. But the hurt doesn't last forever. Love does. And if it were love —in the sense of healthy, stable love and not the emotional, staggering one that you found yourself in —then you both would have stayed. You would have.

You would have tried to make it work because the problems wouldn't have been bigger than the relationship. The problems wouldn't have been so bad that there was no option other than a way out of the relationship. But the problems *were* bad. You both reached a place of such darkness that the only way to see the light was to de-tangle yourselves from each other —which you did. So, maybe they were the best thing that ever happened to you but maybe they weren't. Because the best things stay. Yes, moments disappear and become memories that you look back on for years afterward. Things vanish or fade away too. But people stay. The ones that matter. The ones that love you. The ones that are meant to be in your life. They stay. So, maybe it hurts right now, and maybe it will for a while too. But you will find your way out of this pain eventually. You will find what was always meant for you.

And we are all just broken guitar strings, waiting to be fixed by those who can strum us in harmony again.

—and often that person is you.

Your Last Day

It's okay to feel low sometimes. It's okay if you don't feel like getting up in the morning or brushing your teeth. It's okay if all you want to do is lay on the couch and watch TV all day. It's okay to feel drained, even though your body isn't tired. It's okay. Believe me. Some days are harder than others, heck, some weeks and months are harder than others and we just have to flow with it. You can't keep pushing yourself. You can't keep forcing yourself to move, go out, be productive or do something —*anything*— rather than nothing at all. There's no harm in being still. There's no harm in pausing for a while, even if it's longer than you wanted. You are not in a race against time. The day will still start tomorrow. The sun will rise. The night will fall. And you will be able to do everything that you have laid aside for now. There is time. Trust me. There is time. And even if there wasn't, even if tomorrow were our last day on earth and today was all you had —it would still be okay to spend it in silence. In your own presence. It would still be okay to be with yourself for as long as you wanted. It would still be okay to be still —even if today was all you had. It would still be okay.

Environment

Some people will always bring you down. It is that simple. For some people your achievements won't matter, your growth won't matter and the new love that has brought vast happiness in your life won't matter. The only thing that they will remember —and remind you of— are your weakest moments where you needed them. They will always see you as that person. As someone who needs their support/validation to live a happy fulfilled life. Some people will point out everything that is wrong with you and wave it off as *'care'* and *'concern'* for you, as *'constructive criticism'* from someone who wants *'the best'* for you. If you have someone like this in your life, then take my advice and remove them. You don't need people who only point out your flaws rather than appreciate the things that make you glow. Even if they don't do it on purpose. Even if they don't realise that they are doing it. If you have told them that it makes you uncomfortable and they still haven't changed —then you need to change your environment to one which doesn't have them around.

Take a Chance

And even if this didn't work —I would be glad that we gave each other a chance. Even if it turned out that we weren't meant to be, I would be happy to give you a glimpse inside my heart, to see my vulnerabilities. Because loving someone doesn't mean taking all their love and having a *'happily ever after',* but living —truly, in every sense. Loving someone means learning. Forgiving. Overcoming challenges and growing in ways you never imagined. Loving someone means taking their hand and climbing up the highest mountain you could think of and adventuring along the way. So, even if it didn't work out and we parted ways —I would be honoured to take that journey with you. Because loving someone means giving them a space inside your heart, without thinking about the consequences or letting your fears overwhelm you and knowing —in every way— that maybe one day they will leave; but their place in your heart will stay forever.

Dear You.

I understand that life gets hard sometimes. Stressful. This constant battle between love and life. You feel empty. You think that the cure to your loneliness is to find someone who will complete you. But you are wrong. Because you need to find yourself before they do. You need to be comfortable in your own skin before you are

In a world where people constantly talk about self-love and self-worth —I would like to remind you how magical it is to love and be loved. Remember the wild emotions of falling in love and the gentle hum of friendship. Remember the twinkly laughter that crackles through the airy hues of summer, and the waft of maple pancakes on Saturday morning breakfasts with your family. Remember how soothing it is to hug your people in every stage of your journey —after the tears of heartbreak or when you're sharing stories. The hugs where you bump into each other in the market. The hugs that overwhelm you because it's been so long. The hugs that are tinged with the waft of goodbye. The hugs that pepper long evenings of togetherness —drenched in music, happiness and food. The hugs that you didn't know you needed until you feel them melt into your bones.

Remember holding hands with the person you love and feeling like you're not alone in this world. Remember turning to your side and seeing their innocent, sleeping face —as though nothing could be purer than the way they embrace the long night and their dreams. Remember the wild holidays with your friends during summers that split the school year in two. Remember the kaleidoscope of adventure, love and family that have been sprinkled throughout your life. In a world where people constantly talk about being alone and finding comfort in your own arms —remember how tender it feels when you find comfort in others too.

Promise Me

Promise me that you will continue to be soft in this stormy world. Promise me that you will let your heart be wild and messy and colourful. Promise me that you will change with every hue of life, even the dark, bruised moments of existence that you don't like as much. Promise me that you will drench your soul in the sun and the rain, and you will moon gaze on starry nights, as you wrap yourself warm with your thoughts. Promise me that you will dream —of every adventure you could possibly think of, of quelling your untamed heart, of finding a home for yourself, of being unafraid. Promise me that you will do whatever it takes to build the life you dream of, that you will take risks, trek mountains of lessons and push yourself out of your comfort zone. Promise me that you will welcome new things —like people, friendship, and every new journey that scares you. Promise me that you won't just love your cosy, golden parts but also the muggy ones. The parts of you that are chaotic and rough around the edges. Promise me that you will take a chance —on this life, and on yourself. Promise me that you will take a chance. Promise me that you will.

Perspective

The one thing that I've learned over the last year is how important it is to maintain a healthy balance in your life. Don't get me wrong —I believe in the hustle just as much as the next person and I strongly encourage following your dreams, but I no longer let my life be led by them. It took losing people for me to understand how important the relationships in my life are. A lot more important than my hustle. It's true. The momentary satisfaction that I experience when I tick off a goal on my list can't compare to the life-long satisfaction and happiness I have experienced —and will continue to experience— from the people in my life. I've spent so many years chasing my goals, working tirelessly, through summer holidays, through my free time, through my weekend and all the invaluable periods in my life that I could've given to those I love —and now when I look back; I realise that those goals weren't going anywhere. They would still be there when I woke up the next day. But I couldn't say the same about the people in my life. I couldn't say the same about the relationships that I formed. I couldn't guarantee that my dreams wouldn't be there the next day, but my loved ones would.

That's when my perspective of life changed forever. When I understood that my purpose will live for as long as I do and I will have tomorrow, and the day after, and the day after to focus on them —for as long as I'm alive. But the people that I love —my family and my friends— they won't be here forever. So, instead of putting off our meeting for *'another day'* or *'another time'*, I focus on investing myself in my loved ones instead. I choose to put them first. I choose to invest my time into building important relationships and to loving and being loved. I choose to pick up the phone and make that visit. I choose to say, *'I'll be there for you'*, and mean it every single time. Because now I know how fleeting life is and how tomorrow is never promised, and rather than living my life in regret because I didn't tell someone I love that I love them —I choose to remind them every day of how important they are to me. Because now I know that when the relationships in my life flourish —everything else does too.

Whether you find the right person or not —you can still be the right person for yourself. You can give yourself the love, care and effort that you expect from the right person. You can pick yourself up whenever you stumble and fall. You can hold your own hand as you face the next challenge in your life. You can spill love into your own heart. You can be there for yourself in every way that the right person can. The truth is, we have to be our own lovers, we have to be our own *everything* before we can let someone else in.

Journeys

I know that you can't understand it. But no matter how hard you try, you are going to hurt at least one person at some point in your life. No matter how much energy you put in trying to do it as nicely as you can, in trying to let them down with as much warmth and kindness as possible, their eyes will tell you all you need to know —that you have hurt their heart in a way you can never understand. And unfortunately, that is the sad truth of life. So, we can't be so hard on ourselves for hurting others just because we know what it feels like to go through pain. Sometimes you have to accept that just as people cause you pain, you are bound to cause them pain too. *And that is okay.* Because at the end of the day, those who hurt you played a part in your journey, and those who got hurt by you gave you a space in theirs.

If I care about someone, I can't help but invest all my time and energy into them. I can't help but show them how much they mean to me. I can't help but let them read my eyes and find everything that I have in my heart for them. I can't help but be there for them. I can't help but be a good friend. I can't help but wait for them, for as long as it takes. I can't help but be this transparent. This honest. I can't help but be this expressive, this emotional, this sensitive. *I just can't help it.* And I don't know any more if it is a blessing or a curse. But all I know is —I just can't help but love them this much without expecting the same amount of love for myself. And when I don't receive any of it in return, I just can't help but break a little with each passing day.

Departure

A person's presence can completely change the current flow of your life, and you don't grasp this until they disappear for a short while or —worse— forever. It's a weird experience, welcoming your daily experiences without a flicker of knowledge that someone who has the power to turn your whole world around will arrive one day. And when they do, your universe is split into two parts —life before them and life after them. Everything that you know, that mattered to you, that you prioritised and valued transforms in such a manner that you forget what life before them was like. There are things that you cherished before they arrived which you forget about until after they leave.

That's why their departure hits you. That's why their departure leaves you feeling empty and unsure. It comes as a sudden shock, like a wave slapping softly against the shore until it overwhelms it. You didn't know how much your life changed and how much you changed when they came because being with them felt as easy as breathing, as calm as rain pattering against the windowsill while you both snuggled indoors, and as comfortable as being with your own soul. That is why departure hurts so much. That's why, when people leave, we are left with a gaping hole inside us which rattles like cold air against our bones —because we don't know how to go on anymore. Because we don't remember what life was like before they arrived, because we only knew a universe where they were by our side and now that they are not here, we don't know how to cope. We don't know how to smile. We don't know how to live anymore.

But you must remember that you lived a whole life before

them just fine, inhaling the soft morning air as the sun beamed on your face, having the same dreams, if not more, and following goals which didn't have them in mind. So, *remember this.* Focus on the life you lived before they arrived and promise me this one thing —even if someone else comes after today, you won't forget your life and you won't change yourself so much that you can't find traces of your heart once they leave.

A person's presence can change the flow of your current life completely, but it's up to you how much you let them change, it's up to you whether you want to give them the reign of your heart. It's up to you. It's only up to you.

Love Me Enough

I'm so tired of having expectations. I'm tired of thinking that those I love will treat me well just because they love me. Of making excuses for them every time they let me down. I'm tired of justifying their poor behaviour. I'm tired of telling myself that things will get better. Of reassuring myself that eventually they will realise how much their actions are hurting me. Eventually they will admit that this isn't how to treat someone you care about. Eventually they will apologise and tell me that they will do better next time. They will be kinder. Softer. More understanding. Because the truth is —no matter how much someone loves you, *they are not you.* They haven't lived in your shoes to understand how you're feeling. And no amount of empathising can give them a glimpse of your trauma or past experiences, and that is just how it is. But it would still be nice to know that they care enough to try. And that is what I'm most tired of. I'm tired of believing that one day someone will love me enough to try for me. One day someone will love me enough to try.

We are not afraid to leave.

We are afraid that when we finally decide to leave, they won't ask us to stay.

Sometimes you make mistakes. It's that simple. Sometimes you make mistakes, do wrong and hurt others and you realise this as you're doing it. You realise how much pain you're causing the other person with your actions, but you can't stop yourself. You just can't. Circumstances are such that not hurting them would lead to so much more discomfort and pain in the future than hurting them right now. And that's the truth. No one is perfect. We are going to hurt other people. We are bound to disappoint them. And I know it feels horrible when you know that you're disappointing someone, but you still carry on with your action anyway. Because you have to. Because the situation is such that not hurting them would be worse. And I guess the only way to look at it would be to accept that you did something wrong and let it teach you. Let it grow you. And let it show you that there will be people in this world who will dislike you because of what you did to them —and as hard as it will be, you will have to accept it in order to move on.

Your Person

Find yourself the kind of person who doesn't try too hard to please you by pretending to be something that they're not. The kind of person who is effortlessly imperfect and doesn't try to hide it from you. The kind of person who is fluently honest about your strengths and your weaknesses and supports you if you want to change or work on them. The kind of person with hard principles and easy suggestions to make your life better, and sometimes this happens just by them being there.

Find yourself the kind of person who not only loves you but respects every particle of your existence. The kind of person who looks at you through deep-set, generous lids with an affection that could envelope you entirely and set you free. The kind of person who admires how beautiful you are —with your big brown eyes and generous thighs, and the small pores that dot your face, with your big soft smile and bedhead, with your sudden emotions and overwhelmingly huge heart. The kind of person who not only accepts each thick layer, and each messy fragment of your being but loves you more and more for it every day. Find yourself the kind of person who pushes you to be better, to do good, to work harder, and to excel in your personal and professional life. The kind of person who wants the best for you and will do everything in their power to support you. The kind of person who believes in you more than you believe in yourself.

Find yourself the kind of person who is your best friend. The kind of person who makes you laugh relentlessly, until your cheeks hurt from giggling so much that you have to press them together with your hands. The kind of person who makes being with them a breeze, where hours pass as though they were minutes when you are together. The kind of person with whom you want to take every adventure, live through every experience, and witness all highs and lows of life. Find yourself an imperfectly perfect person, the kind of person who teaches you about love, life, friendship, peace and so much more. Because once you have this person in your life —you will never be scared to love again.

Healing is easier when you open your eyes, and heart, to people who shine with light, because theirs is easier to get through. The kind of light that doesn't care whether there is darkness inside you because it will shine through anyway. The right people quell the ache in your heart without realising it. The right people believe in you, pushing you to believe in yourself and love yourself more and more each day. The right people bring a storm of sunshine, love, and laughter into your life. The right people cause your heart to rattle with happiness. The right people bring you hope. Because healing is inevitable. The characteristic remedial powers of time will ensure that your heart mends itself slowly, yet surely. But with the right people in your life, healing becomes an adventure that you take with those that you love the most —the kind of adventure that no one wants to go on alone— because life, with all its messiness, is a lot more beautiful when others are by your side.

This year taught me that everything is temporary. Our daily routine. Our drive. Our jobs. Education. Exercise. Outings. Our relationships. Everything that we are used to taking for granted, everything that we thought would last forever is just a fleeting moment in the bigger picture that we are mere blips in. This year has taught me how busy we get in our lives —often as meaningless as those of machines in factories— that we ignore all the things that truly matter. Like humanity. Like compassion. Love. Forgiveness. Fighting for what is right. Acting. Believing in change and becoming it for as long as we can to stimulate some sort of growth. It took the whole world ripping at the seams for us to —pause. Breathe. Reflect. And accept that there is so much wrong with the world, and how we will make countless excuses to avoid thinking about the wrongness. To push it to the side. But it took pausing, breathing, and reflecting to understand that *we are the problem*. We are what is wrong with the world. And now is the time to act and do what is right for us all. This year has taught me so much but perhaps the biggest lesson I learned was that the phrase —*'A single person can change the world'*— brings with it a lot more pain that I thought it would.

—the year 2020

Ways to put yourself first this year:

1. Make a list of priorities.

2. Learn to say *'no'* and mean it.

3. Catch up regularly with friends that make you happy.

4. Eat healthy nutritious food.

5. Put away your phone.

6. Start a journal.

7. Read a book/listen to music.

8. At the end of the day, share 3 things that you are grateful for or write them down.

9. Remind yourself that you are worthy as often as you can.

Welcome The Light

How many of you didn't know certain things about yourself until you discovered them after spending a few hours with a new friend or going on holiday with your family/close ones? Then, suddenly you came across a trait that you never knew you had. It's like you have to go through new experiences to know how you would respond to them. You need to taste unfamiliar food to find out what your favourite cuisine is. You need to press your feet in the sand and jump into the ocean to learn about how good it feels. You need to laugh at a few jokes before you discover more about your humour. You need to meet people, talk about life, philosophy and politics to know what your views on those matters truly are. You need to feel happiness like never before to recognise what it means to you and how much you want it in your life. And you need to feel pain on the hands of people that you will accept you don't need going forward. You need to fall head over heels in love with the wrong person to know what it is like when you fall for the right one. And sometimes you need to go through the darkest moments in your life, so when they pass —you want to truly welcome the light.

You Lived

Try to recall the number of times you told yourself that you will *'never be happy again'* but —weeks or months later— you found the corners of your thin lips slowly twirling up into a grin so soft you couldn't even see it. Try to recall the friends who felt like sunshine on the darkest days of your life, friends who you thought would be by your side forever —but you never noticed how the threads weakened as time wore on until they were nothing but a bundle of memories of a moment long gone. But you lived. Even though it felt like your life would never be the same without them —you made new friends, took different adventures, and uncovered the hues of living that you had not with them. Try to recall that instance in your healing when you told yourself that it was all over, that you would never stop hurting. That this was it. This pain, these pieces of your heart that were strewn across the floor —you would never be able to sow them back together again. But before you realised it, you were healing again. Those parts of you somehow found their way back to each other and welcomed newer pieces that made you, *you*.

Try to recall the number of times you've nearly given up, or moments in your life when someone's hurt you so much that you can feel the pain through your ribs. Try to recall the hurting, the arguments and the joys. Your life has been a kaleidoscope of emotions, healing and learning —and it has been beautiful. It has truly been beautiful. So, stop telling yourself that you want to give up now. Stop telling yourself that this time it feels too real. Because that is how it felt before. You thought that you would die because of the pain. But you lived. You lived.

There is nothing worse than loving someone who never realised what they had when they were with you, and letting them go for their sake because *they felt that they deserved more.*

My Younger Self

I would tell my younger self that things get easier with time, and that life isn't always going to be this tough, or bitter, or difficult to get through. Life isn't always going to resemble a bursting grey cloud ready to shower you with pain. Yes, there will be a little bit of rain —but the sunshine will always follow. I would tell my younger self that all those tears aren't useless at all. They will make you stronger. More capable. Self-sufficient. More able. Those tears will purify your soul —truly, they will. Your tears will build an ocean of healing that you will set sail on to become the person that you were always meant to be. I would tell my younger self that hope is what keeps us going, and it will keep you going too. It will push you to fight and fight and fight until your hands are permanently balled up by your sides and there is nothing that you can't deal with. Hope will give you the strength to move on —from heartbreaks and broken friendships, from failure and loss and all kinds of hurt that you will witness as you grow older. I would tell my younger self to hold on to this hope during the darkest, grimmest moments in life —because that is what will shape you.

I would tell my younger self to keep moving forward. To never give up. To have faith in your tremendous soul and the love that bubbles within it. To believe in all your dreams for the future and work towards them. As hard as you can. As loyally as you are capable of. And to never set yourself any limits or barriers. I would tell my younger self to never be afraid of all the hurdles set before you, because that pounding heart inside you knows with certainty that you have the power to change your life forever. I would tell my younger self that love is gentle. It is healing. Love is easy. Love doesn't question you. It doesn't bring you to your knees. It doesn't hold you in a limbo. Love sets you free. And that is the only kind of love that you should accept in your life. Love is not a hard rock jammed inside your chest. It is not hot tears spiralling down your cheeks. It is not angry or mean or sore to your soul. I would remind my younger self that if love isn't healthy for you —then it is better to protect yourself by never having loved at all.

Sometimes we think that life isn't in our favour because what we really wanted hasn't worked out. But that is when we need to have utmost faith that everything happening at that particular moment is not only in our favour but it's what is meant for us. And it might not make sense to us right then, or even weeks and months down the line. But one day we will look back at this time and be grateful that what we wanted *didn't happen.* Because on that day we will understand that not only did everything work out for the best, but that it always does. It has to.

Love That Stays

I hope you meet someone who is unafraid to tell you how they feel. Someone who looks at you with a vulnerable gaze as their emotions spill out of their heart into yours. I hope you meet someone who means it when they say, *'I love you'*. Someone who is all actions and honest gestures rather than excuses and silence. Someone who is generous with everything that they do for you. I hope you meet someone who doesn't think twice before picking up the phone to call you and apologise —even if it wasn't their fault. Someone who puts their ego aside so they can put your relationship first. I hope you meet someone who has no boundaries when it comes to their love and respect for you, but also knows where to draw the line if you're testing their patience. I hope you meet someone who is as crazy about starry nights and wild adventures as they are about you. Someone who loves last-minute plans and hikes up sun-dipped hills, someone who secretly cries during sad movies and gets upset when you don't say *'I love you'* before you cut the phone. I hope you meet someone who isn't perfect but tries hard to be a better person for themselves, and for you. Someone who accepts that relationships aren't easy —but they choose to work on this one over and over again. I hope you meet someone who never gives up on you, no matter what. I hope you meet someone who means it when they say that they will stay.

Adventures

Fill your life with adventures. With picnics on a hilly park that dips into the sunset and a bright brunch with your loved ones. Fill your life with good people. With people who are warm on your soul. With people who can fill your cracks with love and friendship in such a way that you forget you were ever broken. You forget there ever was a time where loving others scared you. Where caring for others scared you. Where trusting others scared you. Fill your life with experiences that make your smile stretch from cheek to cheek. With moments that you can remember even as memories of the years become weak. Moments where you can hear the music in the background of cackles and shared stories, where looking at old photos causes a softness to rise inside your chest because you know just how special that day was. Moments where memories of every adventure make you tingle with nostalgia. Fill your life with love. The kind that comes in the form of good hearts and soft words, the kind that stands by your side and doesn't give up on you. Fill your life with everything that you ever wanted and watch how those very things give you a journey of a lifetime.

I no longer look for validation in others.

My validation comes from within.
My worth comes from within.

Time to Heal

Maybe right now is not about you finding love —but finding yourself. Maybe this moment in your life is about journeying through your experiences alone because that is how you will grow and be comfortable in your skin. Maybe right now it's not about *'two'* but *'you'*. Unashamedly imperfect and growing *'you'*. The *'you'* that has gone through more in a few years than some have their entire lives. The *'you'* that has faced enough hardship for lifetimes of learning and evolving, for lifetimes of trying to move away from that trauma and finding tenderness in the cold happiness that will follow. Because it really is like that sometimes. Sometimes life puts you against so much that even the happy moments after are tinged with a bitter-sweet regret of what you lost. Of how much you lost. Sometimes happiness isn't just happiness —it's a mixture of healing and pain. It's a mesh of every single person who touched you and everyone who one day will. Sometimes happiness isn't having fun at that moment but knowing that after everything —*after it all*— you still have the courage to smile. And sure, it would be nice to have someone to share the pain with. It would be nice to turn to another so your pain can become bearable. It would be nice to cry on someone's shoulder as you offload about everything that you are going through.

But maybe right now is not the time for love but for healing. For growth. Maybe right now is the time for you to become whole in every single way. Maybe right now you are not supposed to find love —even though it would be nice to have someone to go through all of this with— but instead, you are supposed to find you. The *'you'* that was lost along the way.

Don't question it. They love you because they see that you are beautiful. They love you because they understand you as much as they need to in order to get a glimpse of your journey, in order to see your growth, in order to witness the softness of your heart and your strength. Don't question it. They love you because you are wonderful. They love you because they see everything that you are worthy of, everything that you don't see in yourself. Don't question it. Just embrace it. They love you *because they do* —that is all. That is all.

You deserve to be loved *for* all your broken pieces,

not *despite* them.

Friendships

Pay attention. Pay attention to those who said, *'I'll always be there for you',* but suddenly —when you are happy in every sense of the word, they're not by your side anymore. Pay attention to their faces when you tell them about the things you achieved, the adventures you went on and the new love you've found in your life. It will tell you everything you need to know. You will finally realise that some relationships are only strong because *you are weak*, and that those friendships last as long as your low points do and the moment you become happy, the moment there is light in your life, the moment you truly accept the sunshine that has come your way —those friendships are nowhere to be found. But this doesn't mean that those relationships weren't real or the moments you spent with them —it just means that your time with them was spent on a stage in your life that brought you sadness. A stage that you couldn't wait to get away from. And the moment you did, the instant that you started to feel better and more whole —those friendships disappeared because they had nothing to fill into anymore. And it's sad. It's truly sad that the strength of some relationships is dependent on how weak you are, but it's the truth. And it is a truth you need to accept if you want to move on from those people rather than let them shackle you to a time that you don't want to go back to.

I Will Love You

I will wake you up with soft kisses each morning. I will try my best not to get irritated when you make fun of me. I will let you burn the pancakes on Saturday mornings and eat them with a smile on my face. I will laugh at all your jokes, even the ones that aren't funny. I won't steal your fries, and I promise that I will always share mine. I won't say *'no'* to seeing you, especially when you're upset. I will let you cuddle me until you feel better. I will join in all your silly antics; jumping over fences, crossing rivers and running in the mud. I will go on as many walks with you as you want, even if the park looks like something out of a horror movie. I will kiss your cheeks, your eyes, and the big grin on your face. I will hear your side of the story —even when I'm angry. I will watch your favourite shows with you. I will go to the game. I will let you decide what we eat for dinner. I won't say anything when you wear the shirt that I don't like. I will hold your hand when you need it the most. I will be there for you. I will kiss you each time you feel alone. I will love you. I will love you.

Memories

Sometimes the memory of an experience doesn't leave —you just learn to live with it. Time is split in half between your life before that event and your life after it and no matter how much you wish you could turn back the clock —you just can't. Sometimes an experience is so life-changing that it causes you to rethink your whole existence and where other people stand in your life, and after that —you can never see anything in the same way again. Sometimes the hurt is so raw that you can't move on from it without leaving a huge chunk of yourself in the past. The only way you can step away from everything that happened is by refusing to think about what was or what could have been and instead, focusing on what is. And the truth is, whatever happened has happened now and you need to learn to live with it. You need to learn to accept it. You need to understand that some things are not meant to be, and rather than letting this break you —let it make you stronger.

Trust Again

I know that you're scared. You're scared to trust someone new because you've been hurt before. You've been shown by those who didn't value your heart how painful it is to put your trust in the wrong person. To rely on the wrong person. To love the wrong person over and over again even when your mind told you that something is amiss. I know that you're scared to put the weight of your faith in someone new when the consequences of loving the wrong person have come before you. But I want you to know that trusting other people isn't a weight that you should carry on your shoulders — because it's on them to gain your trust. It's on them to show you that they deserve your utmost faith. It's on them to be as honest as they can, so when the time comes to hand them your trust —it doesn't feel like you're burdening them, or that they are burdening you. Instead, it feels easy. Comfortable. As though you are merely sharing your space with them rather than your trust. I know that you're scared to let new people in when in the past things haven't gone so great. And you're right in your place to feel this way.

But think about it this way —when you fail a test you revise harder and try your best to pass it the next time, don't you? In the same way, when someone breaks your trust, you just have to focus on the many signals why that happened, and the next time you think about trusting someone again —revise harder on your self-worth and your relationship to make sure that they deserve the trust that you hand them. And when you do give them the weight of your trust —accept that they earned it. Accept that you have done everything you could in your power to protect yourself and give them the chance to protect you.

If the person that you love is constantly making mistakes and taking you for granted, then there is something wrong with them and not you.

And if they can't keep up with their promises, then darling —*they are the ones who have failed you.*

Stop putting into others more than what they put into you. Stop being readily available, eager to talk to, and going out of your way to do things for others when they will not do the same. Stop saying *'yes'* to everything and start saying *'no'* to protect yourself. Start demanding that they give you time. Start holding your heart tightly against your chest rather than carrying it in your palms, ready to share with everyone that you love. Start asking for care in return, for love in return, for time in return. Stop saying *'it's okay'* when they cancel on you again. Stop forgiving them when they say hurtful things because *'I know they didn't mean it'*. Stop making excuses for others and start putting yourself first. Stop spoon-feeding love to people who won't make half the effort with you. Stop being the one who calls first, who texts first, who makes the plans and goes out of their way to do things for them. Start taking a step back. Let them call you. Let them text you. Let them realise that you won't be there forever, showering them with affection and kindness. Let them make effort with you. And start accepting that you're being taken for granted —and don't let them get away with it. Take a stand. Tell them how you feel. Let them take care of you for once.

Stages

I was speaking to a friend the other day who said something that stuck with me; *'Why do other people have it so easy?'*, she said, *'It seems like no matter how hard my pain is, it always falls short in comparison to their happiness'.* And I thought about this, a lot. Growing up I had seen more than enough pain, struggle, and tears. And I can't deny that I didn't ask myself the same question more than once. It seemed like I had received everyone's share of pain while they got more happiness than I could have ever imagined. They always looked like they were having a much better time than I was —with their family, friends and personal life. Everything worked out for them fine, while those very things had fallen apart more than once in my life. And truthfully, I can't tell you how I dealt with it at the time, because when you're witnessing that moment—*your pain hits the deepest.*

But now, after years of healing, I can say I have accepted that people will be in different stages of their lives at the same time. That stage in my life was one of growth. It demanded so much from me that I would not be who I am without it. But maybe the stage they were on was one of love and joy, and as much as I questioned why they were so happy while I was suffering —would I have said the same if I was happy and they were in pain? Would I want to be in their shoes when they went through the hardest moments of their life? If not, then why did I want to be in their shoes when they were in the happiest?

And this changed my life. Understanding that journeys towards happiness are filled with thorns of pain and heartache that people tread on for years before they reach a place of light, and learning that if you aren't willing to travel those difficult journeys instead of others, then you can't compare your darkest moments to their brightest. Because one day you will be in the happiest part of your journey that others might compare themselves to —but they won't know how many thorns it took to get there.

Race

Life isn't a race and other people are not your competition. Although it might seem like you need to be on their level in terms of your personal achievements, career, and love life — because you both came from the same place— that's not true. You don't need to run at the speed of those around you, especially when your circumstances are different. You need to focus on your own journey. On your own path. On the goals that you've have set for yourself and the personal obstacles that you need to face. If other people are doing well in their life —congratulate them. Be happy for them. Give them a pat on the back and move on. Don't let it affect you. Don't let their happiness eat away at yours. Don't get upset because you haven't crossed those very milestones yet. Just focus on your individual path. Pay attention to what you need to do to manifest the life that you want, and compare your present to your past, not anyone else's —and that's when you will realise nothing else matters apart from focusing on your own journey.

Moments

And it is this exact moment that you will look back on and miss the most. This existing. This being able to wake up in the morning and knowing that —no matter how crippling your life can sometimes feel— you still have the choice to change the direction of your journey. It is this exact moment in your life that you will miss the most. This package of time *before* the heavy responsibilities and *after* the yesteryears of innocence —the one where you can do and be whatever you want. It's this precise time in your life —where you can go on long hikes, sunbathe on the beach or spend a day just existing in front of the TV without a care in the world about anything. It's being able to take off for a week without the responsibilities of kids or a family that you will miss the most. It's being able to hop into a café for hours on end with your book and a coffee that you will miss the most. It's being able to call your friends to meet up without having to plan it weeks in advance that you will miss the most. It is this moment, this spontaneity of life that you take for granted so often that you will miss the most.

So, enjoy it as much as you can. Look around and let the gratefulness exhale through you as you come to terms with how temperamental life is. And how often the things we take for granted can be changed in an instant —making us wish we could have appreciated it just that little bit more. Because one day you will look back at everything good that happened in your life and say to yourself *'I wish I could go back and do it all over again',* and it will be this moment, this exact moment in your life that you will miss the most.

Things won't get better straightaway. Especially when you experience heartbreak, lose friends and relationships, or live in a broken home. Especially when you experience the kind of pain where you empty out the contents of your life's happiness into an ocean of despair and don't know how to come through from it. Things take time and this time could be anywhere between months and years —so, please be gentle with yourself. Be kind. You will get to where you are supposed to be one day, but remember —you always receive the happiness that you deserve *when you are meant to*. Not when it is too early and not when it is too late. Only when the time is right. So, be patient with the plan that is set for you. You will receive your share of everything when you are meant to.

You are so lucky because you were able to drag yourself
out of a toxic love that is sinking me like quicksand.

This Kind of Love

You deserve an 'I'll put you first and nothing else matters' kind of love. A 'lift your feet off the ground every time that we hug' kind of love. A 'pick you up from the front door and take you for a spontaneous drive' kind of love. You deserve a 'book your favourite movie and sneak in the snacks' kind of love. A 'hold your hand tight when I'm driving' kind of love. A 'we can argue but I won't let you sleep without saying goodnight' kind of love. You deserve a 'here's the meds, a soup and a hug 'cos you're sick' kind of love. A 'we'll work through everything together' kind of love. An 'I'll never give up on you' kind of love. A 'love that gets stronger with each passing day' kind of love. You deserve a 'happens once in a lifetime but changes your life forever' kind of love.

Let Down

Do you ever feel like you've let everyone down? Like, no matter what you do —someone will be disappointed in you. I spoke to a friend about this the other day, and I felt my shoulders sag, as though a weight had been lifted off them when the words finally left me; *'I'm so tired of trying to please everyone'*. As though my simply saying it was enough to relieve the pressure of living it. And the one thing I learned from that conversation was this —people will always feel slightly disappointed at something that you've done. No matter what it is. Even if you try to be your best self in every way, you can't be because you're not perfect. And their expectations of you will never align with who you truly are because perhaps they've put you on a pedestal that you don't want to be on. A pedestal that doesn't take into account the mistakes you might make and the emotions you will feel throughout your journey. I've learned through wanting to do what's right that *I can't get it right all the time.* I won't be able to. So, instead of trying to please everyone around me —I need to please my morals and my heart instead. And if that means sometimes hurting others because I've let them down —then that's fine. Because that is way better than pushing myself every day to please others and *still failing to*, because on those days, even though I have let others down — I feel like I've let myself down the most.

Red Signals

Don't ignore the red signs that blare at you when someone treats you a certain way. Read their words and understand their actions. If they are doing something that indicates that they don't care —believe them. People who don't make effort to understand or listen to you *don't want to*. It is that simple. Yes, I understand that some people are going through things in their life that make it difficult for them to love you as much as you love them. For them to care about you. But this is different to someone who has always treated you badly. It's different to someone whose words have never been encouraging or kind or gentle to your heart. And I also understand that some people aren't good with words —but if they aren't good with their actions either then the truth is they probably don't value you the way that you do. They probably don't need you in their life. They probably have other priorities that don't take your happiness into consideration and —as much as it hurts— you have to make the decision to remove yourself from them.

Don't ignore the red flags. The signs that tell you they don't love you back or even like you enough to make you stay. Don't ignore the flags that make you question whether they care. Listen to their words. Trust their actions. If they are treating you badly time and time again —believe that they don't want you in their life as much as you do. Then welcome that truth entirely. Completely. And after you've accepted that their behaviour is as good as their words —think about what you need to do next, but remove yourself from that situation before it becomes too difficult to.

Maybe the laws of nature fight for some people to end up together. Maybe you are meant to be together at some point in your lives but right now is not the time. Maybe you will find your way back to them or maybe they will. And no matter how much you try to fight it, no matter how much you tell yourself that it will never work —*it does*. Because it has to. Because your souls belong together like two roads headed in the same direction, no matter how far apart they are. But the point is that this can't happen without the growth and healing that is destined for you both. The point is that right now is not the right time because you haven't done the necessary individual work that you need to before you come together. And sure, you won't know whether your soul is going to find theirs again, but during the hurting and the moving on —you will grow more than you've ever grown before. So, when you do find them again —it won't be like old times, no. It will be a new experience altogether. It will be a brand-new journey and a different adventure that your heart now can't witness because it's so broken. But when it comes together, when it heals, *God, when it heals,* and you meet again —it will be a love like no other. And maybe you both are meant to be, but you won't know that when you're hurting. *And maybe you aren't meant to be* —because that is a possibility. An honest one that the hope in your heart can't ignore forever. But still, take the journey. Accept the growth and welcome the healing. Because it will change you in ways you never imagined. It will change the course of your life forever. It will add new shades of friendship, adventure, and purpose in your life. And in the end, it will give you the love and happiness that you're deserving of. It will. Believe me —it will.

Too Much

And some people will look at you and the way you see the world, the way you speak to people and the way you treat others, then —after observing everything and judging every part of you— they will tell you that you're being *'too nice'*, as if it is an insult. You need to remember that you're not being *'too nice'* —you're simply being human in a world filled with people who have long forgotten humanity.

Losing Everything

Sometimes, it doesn't work out and this ends up being the best thing that could happen to you. Sometimes the *'right person'* was the wrong one all along, but you didn't realise this until they left. You didn't acknowledge how chaotic they were for your heart until you looked back at the weeks, months and years that you spent together. You couldn't distinguish the red signs from their behaviour until after you removed them from your life. You see the signs later. The messiness. The excuses. The inconsistency. The false promises. Everything becomes as clear as day after you take off the blurry lens through which you were seeing them the whole time. Sometimes they need to leave for you to know their worth, and sometimes they need to leave for you to understand yours. And it is okay. Because sure, you won't get the time that you spent with them back but what you will get is this —clarity. Certainty of what you're looking for. Recognition of your worth. A sense of happiness that you never received with them by your side, or even if you did receive it —it vanished as quickly as it arrived. What you will get is this —bundles of lessons and growth. You will get an understanding of what love is and what it isn't. A vision of what you want your future relationship to look like. A purpose. New dreams and lots of hope. Sometimes it takes losing everything you once loved to find everything that is good for you. Sometimes it takes losing it all to find it all over again.

Only You

There is no one else my heart chooses to beat for. It is only you. I could travel and search the ends of the earth, but I still won't find another you. And it is so crazy to know this when a few years ago you were a mere figment of my imagination, a dream that I had for a future that seemed so distant. So far away. But here you are —loving me in every hue of the sun. Here you are, falling so effortlessly into me and letting me see how golden warm another person's arms can be. Here you are, giving me the confidence to choose myself over and over again, without guilt, without fear of losing you, without any false concern that choosing me somehow means not choosing you. There is no one else I would rather spend the rest of my days with. Watching the sun bounce into another starry night. Tossing stories, smiles, and hugs over a net of friendship, trust, and love that we have built together. Working hard towards our dreams and believing in this foundation of *us*. There is no one else for me other than you. Believe me. There is no one else.

Appreciate the battles you have won and the ones you
have lost. Because throughout all the losses and gains
—you found yourself in countless ways.

Right Person

With the right person, life is an adventure. It is a journey that you will happily take, no matter how uneven, edgy, and uncertain it is —as long as you have them by your side. With the right person, no goal is too hard to reach, no hurdle is too high to jump, and no dream is too scary to pursue. With the right person, happiness rises in every corner of your life, and you become overwhelmed with the courage to take risks, to do what's right for you, and to not accept less than what you deserve from anyone. With the right person —you grasp your true worth. You understand that your value rests not in the tongues of those who will never be able to measure your magnificence, but in the lines that pattern your palms, marking your destiny.

With the right person, you start to believe in yourself, in your dreams, your plans and your hopes for the future. With the right person, your hard work doesn't lessen but becomes worthwhile because you see a light flickering in the distance, indicating that you aren't too far off from your destiny. The right person makes you believe that you can achieve anything. With the right person, you shine in every part of your life. You smile more, you laugh wholeheartedly, you glow from every inch, every arch and corner and you feel love bubble inside your heart. With the right person, you feel calm, satisfied, and relaxed. With the right person, you finally feel at home. When love is good for you, when it is truly healing —you become wealthy in the way that matters the most.

Your Life

The truth is, most people won't understand the life that you live, and frankly —you won't understand theirs. They might look at you and your dreams and goals as an alien-language that no amount of interpretation could translate. And that will be fine. Because that is what being unique is all about. That is what being an individual consists of —creating your own dreams and goals, forming relationships, and finding joy in the small things that might not make sense to anyone else but you. Because you live your life for you. You live your life to make sense of all your experiences combined and still find happiness in them. You live your life to adventure and soar and heal as you push forward, and they live their lives for them. The truth is, not everyone will agree with the choices that you make and the goals you seek —but if it makes sense to you, if it drives you, if it brings you comfort then you've done the most important thing of all; you've made sense of your own life, despite all the odds. And that, in itself, is beautiful.

A lot of us fall in and out of what we thought was love but is nothing other than our past trauma staring back at us, and still —we refuse to accept a positive and healthy version of love in our lives. And that is what's wrong with us. If you're growing into a strong-willed individual, if you've started affirming your worth and if you're changing in considerable ways —*then let love change with you.* Into something positive. Into something good. Don't let all the other aspects of your life grow with you while love is still that fragile, tender thing that cause you so much pain in the past. The good thing about love growing with you is this —as everything else in your life falls into place, love does too.

Yes. I'm scarred.

But my scars make me who I am.

The scrawny, shadowed lines, crimson in the middle and brown at the edges, remind me of the things I have experienced and how far I have come, and their fading boundaries are evidence of my strength to move on, come what may.

Best Friend

Heartbreaks that result from losing your best friend hurt just as much, if not more. Because how can they not? When your best friend has been there for you through all the mugginess, the pain, the arguments, and slivers of uncertainty —it's hard to picture a life with them not by your side. It's tough, losing family or friends. It's hard no longer having those people who have been through thick and thin with you, who laughed and cried with you, who held your hand during problems that they might not have understood. *But they understood you.* They worried about you. And that is what mattered the most. And when the seasons change, and life turns a new shade —living without those who love you becomes difficult. Leaving behind best friends who went through everything with you feels like a wound that will never heal. And perhaps it never truly does. Because every person who comes into your life makes a special place for themselves that no one else can fill. That is why losing your best friend feels like you have lost a huge part of you. You made promises of forever but now it feels like you have a single ticket to a life trip that you had planned for two.

Love as much as your heart lets you. Do it. Don't be afraid to love others and let them love you. But know that with loving comes the potential for getting hurt. With loving comes the responsibility of giving them your trust and earning theirs. With loving comes sharing —your friends, your dreams, your family, your future and your entire lives if it's what you want. So, yes —love is beautiful. It is life changing. It is magical and wonderful and everything that you ever imagined. But it isn't easy. It isn't a walk in the park. It isn't all the good parts of your favourite romance movie minus-the-bad. It just isn't. But I would still say that you should love as much as your heart lets you. Because as they say, it's better to have lived and loved —even if it means getting hurt— than to never have loved at all.

3 false beliefs about relationships:

Your partner needs to be your best friend —it's unhealthy to rely on your partner as your only source of contact, support, and encouragement. A healthy relationship is one where there is a balance of positive interaction with your partner but also enough space to let you both interact with others and gain invaluable support from there.

A healthy relationship does not have any disagreements —you are two individuals with a different set of upbringing, morals, worldview, and experiences that have contributed to the people that you have become. Inevitably, you will want one thing and they will want another. You're bound to disagree on matters and argue. In a healthy relationship, you both actively want to communicate and resolve those problems in order to reach a happier place together.

A relationship is the cure to all my problems —a relationship won't solve/cure your problems. Your partner is not a therapist, and they shouldn't have to *'fix'* you in any way. Those problems will still be there. Your fears will still be there. Your trauma and learning and the need for growth will be there. Because your partner was never supposed to fix those things for you anyway —*you were.*

I feel devoid of emotions these days. My heart is empty, my mind numb, my thoughts are drifting into various corners, and this soul feels much heavier than it did before. I don't know if this is a sign of peace, or the sign of a storm brewing inside me.

You can't change everyone. Some people will treat you badly and there's nothing you can do other than remove yourself from that situation. Not everyone is going to be kind. Not everyone has a heart like you. Some people have been taught more about hurting others than healing them and instead of taking this as a burden on your part —let it go. It's not on you to teach everyone to be nice to you. But it is your responsibility to detach yourself from those who can't respect you or treat you well. You can't change everyone, but you can certainly change the people you surround yourself with and give value to. So, do something about that part of your life instead.

Happiness

I am happy. It is weird to say these three words and truly mean them. But, for the first time in a long time, I feel this in my soul. A soft, subtle tingle forms in my heart when I wake up each morning because I no longer hurt as I used to. A smile plays on my lips when I realise that I'm not waiting for anyone's messages with my phone plopped eagerly in my palm, as I used to; my eyes lingering in its direction every time I received a notification. I am happy in the way that matters —with an aura of delicate ease all around me, enough to protect me from all the negative thoughts that would play in my mind before. And I finally accept that I am happy because I want to be —because I know that I deserve it— and that is what changed.

Chasing Love

Don't chase feelings. Stop looking for potential in others. Stop telling yourself that they will make more effort, or they will change, or they will start taking your emotions seriously and for once —*just once*— listen to what your gut tells you. Stop ignoring the reality that hammers in your mind every time they say something cutting, or when the red signals flash before your eyes and, instead of listening to them, you let your vision be blurred by feelings so strong that you can't see what's right or wrong anymore. Stop chasing love. Because if love was meant to be chased then we wouldn't fall into it, we just wouldn't. If love was meant to be chased, then it would be another one of those things that we need to tick off our list. If love was one of your goals that needed to be achieved, then once you experienced it —just like every other contingent goal— you would want something else. You would want someone else. You would want the next high for a short while. The next challenge. The next thing. But love is not a thing. Love is not a challenge.

Love is not a goal. It's not a drug, no matter what anyone says. It's not a fleeting feeling. It's not something that needs to be pursued. It's an emotion that is felt. It's an adventure that you fall into. Deeply. Irrevocably. It's a commitment. It's a choice. An action. It's a promise that you make to someone —one that stays forever. And this promise can't be one-sided, it can't be made to someone that you find potential in, it can't be made when the love just isn't there.

Stop chasing feelings. Stop chasing love. Just let it be. What is meant for you will find its way to you, trust me —it will.

Nothing stays the same. People move on. Hearts break. Dreams change. What you wanted from life vs. what is important to you now varies as time goes on. Friends move cities and relationships change shades as though they were setting with the sun. And all you can do is accept each phase of life with open arms and try to make the most of who you were and who you have become.

Living. Loving. Learning.

Sometimes I don't know how to express what I feel, want or need from my life. It genuinely feels like I don't know what I'm doing anymore. All I know is that I wake up in the morning, have breakfast and try to get through the day as best as I can. It may look like I've got everything figured out. It may look like I know what I'm doing. I have goals. Ambitions. Places to be. People to meet. Meetings to attend. But genuinely —I'm as lost as any other sane person. And that's okay. In this ever-changing world it may seem like we all need to have our lives put together, or a plan for the future —but that's not true. We don't need to plan our days/weeks in advance. We can just live. In the moment. As we are. We can choose to make the most of what life gives us and be grateful for it. We can try. To be happier. Softer. Kinder. Gentler with ourselves. And even if we make mistakes —we can start again. And we can keep going. Living, loving, and learning all over again.

And there will be some regrets that we will carry in our hearts forever. Moments in our live where we were the weakest that flash before our eyes suddenly, out of nowhere. Memories of a time where we wish we could have said something, or nothing, or done things differently so the consequences wouldn't have been what they are now. Some regrets are so heavy on our souls that they never really leave us —they just become really good at hiding. They stay dormant. Silent. Quiet through the good and bad days that follow until they surprise us while we're driving home or washing the dishes, or when we're enjoying ourselves until they come back like a stabbing wound —hurting us. Making our heart rattle. Causing us to shy away with disappointment. There will be some regrets that we wish we could have done something about. Moments in our lives where we wish we could have spoken loudly or spoken at all so that person didn't leave. Or that relationship didn't give up on us. Or that family member who we wish we could have seen more of didn't think that we never loved them before they left. Because we did. Because we do. Because we always will.

Unhappy Hearts

Sometimes, no matter how hard we try —we can't be truly happy for others because of everything that's going on in our own lives. In moments like these, even a small bout of joy in their lives plunges us into further darkness, into the hole that we find ourselves incapable of getting out of. It's hard, it's unbelievably hard to tell yourself that, *'Everything will be okay',* when all the plans that you had made for yourself have done a U-turn. And when those very plans fall in place for those you genuinely care about —you wonder whether something is wrong with you. You question your life. Your actions. You question all the decisions that led you to where you are today. And when you're jealous or miserable as things fall into place for those very people —you think even worse of yourself. How could you feel like this? How could you not bring yourself to be happy for someone who would celebrate all your joys with you?

The first thing you need to accept in moments like this is that you're not a bad person. Feeling miserable in light of other people's happiness is a way of coming to terms with what's wrong with your life. And once you've figured out that *something is wrong with your life* —you need to take the necessary actions to make a change. Yes, you can't control how you feel about certain things but what you can do is correct the circumstances that led to those feelings to begin with. And the most important thing of all —you need to understand that every person is on a journey of their own. Maybe other people have reached the milestones that you had set for yourself, and they probably didn't witness the pain or the negative experiences that you did. Maybe the stages that led them to these bouts of happiness were softer than the thorns of healing that you had to experience. But it doesn't mean that they didn't witness their own struggles. Their individual pain. It doesn't mean that they didn't have to cross difficult hurdles to get to where they are. So, stop comparing your journey to theirs. The lessons you learnt along the way built you into the person you are today and the things that they learned will build them. And I know that you feel guilty if you're not genuinely happy for them —but this is normal human behaviour. Focus on why you're feeling that way and then try to take something from it. Grow. Get inspired by those very people. Make the right choices and change your life for the best.

Those very feelings that are bringing darkness into your life —turn them into important tools that can lead you towards the light.

Loving Someone

I guess you don't realise how selfless you can be until you love another person. Whether it's your parents, siblings or a partner —loving other people brings out the best in you. It allows you to see your true humanity and how much warmth you have within your heart for others. It shows you your true self —the one that is willing to go to any lengths to make the people they love happy. I didn't know how much seeing others hurt would cause me pain either until I started loving them —*entirely*. I realised then that love isn't just the balm to our pain, but it is also the thread that links our hearts together. A thread that, if pulled in either direction, can affect us both. A thread that can sow our pieces back together without us noticing but can also rip us apart because of the smallest problem. The thing is, you can't fathom how easy it is to put someone else first until you start loving them. Because suddenly their happiness becomes yours. Their pain becomes yours. Their dreams and hopes for the future become yours. Everything that has the potential to go good or bad in their life is imprinted in your head to such a degree that it is almost as though those are your fears and your insecurities. And I guess you don't realise it beforehand. Because you never expected that loving someone meant putting their life before your own.

Meant for You

The people who are meant to be in your life will find their way back to you. They have to. Because the laws of nature have decided that maybe this time was not yours, maybe this moment was not meant for love but for something else. Maybe these stages of both your lives are there to prepare you for different battles —but you will come together again. You will learn, grow, heal and perhaps even love others before you find your way back to each other. Before the years have spilled into the crevices of your journeys and you have so much to catch up on, so much to learn about each other that you missed out on. Before they realise that the *'you'* they left behind is no longer the *'you'* they find —because of the different shades of growth you experienced. The people who are meant for you, the ones whose journey takes them on a new course altogether, will find you again. Because there is nowhere else for them to go. Because they can trek down as many stormy paths as they are meant to, but they will still not find the home that they had made with you. Because you both have to learn, change and mend into the right people for each other. The people who are meant for you will travel to the edges of the earth and still come back to you. Because they have to. They do.

Show me love. You don't need to hold me close. You don't need to whisper it in my ear. You don't need to kiss me under the stars, and you don't need to always be here.

Just look into my eyes and show me love.

Everything happens for a reason, and I didn't believe in this much before I got hurt in possibly the worst way. I did think that certain things were predestined, but I refused to accept that hurting could contribute to my growth to this extent. But when I was laughing with friends around a makeshift campfire, years after I had a few horrible experiences, feeling nothing but a soft dewy warmth in my heart —I was finally able to understand how far I had come. And not far in terms of age or goals but in terms of growth. Learning. Healing. You see, there was a time in my life where my pain was a dark tunnel with no light at the end, where my trauma was the heavy grey cloud that followed me no matter how kind the sunshine was. But then, I began to heal. To change. To take more from my experiences than I had before. And that is when I realised —it was all meant to be. Sure, I made some decisions that contributed to transforming my life after the low points —but I could never have seen the light if it didn't exist to begin with. God, a higher reality, the laws of nature —they saved me. It was then that I accepted that everything happens for a reason. All the hurting. The pain. The lost friendships. The heartache. Even the loves that we don't see coming and the ones we didn't expect would leave. They are all playing a part in the journey that is about our growth, our healing, and our life. A journey that is about us. And even though it may seem like those experiences were bigger than us, that those people were more important —we were the main character in this story all along. Not them. They were just passers-by. Tools for our learning. Instruments that quickened our growth somehow. But it was never about them. It was never about them. Because at the end of it —the story was ours all along.

Other people can't put your pieces back together. They can't fix you. They can't heal your past trauma or somehow fight all your battles for you. You need to stop looking for answers in them. You need to stop believing that love will save you. You have to understand that you are the only way out of this mess that you find yourself in. You have to believe that nothing others will say or do can fix your problems. And you need to let go —of seeking their validation, of relying on those around you, of believing that maybe, just maybe, everything will work out if you continue to search for answers in others. They don't have the answers that you're looking for. Love does not have the solution. If you want to find a way to solve your problems —look within yourself because that is where you will find it.

Ways to take better care of yourself:

Physical self-care —eat healthy nutritious food, keep active (go on walks + step away from your desk), and get 8 hours of sleep each night.

Social self-care —surround yourself with people (family, friends, and colleagues) who contribute to your wellbeing.

Psychological self-care —carry out activities that stimulate your mind i.e., books, podcasts, documentaries, puzzles etc.

Emotional self-care —develop ways to better express how you feel to yourself and your close ones. Try to understand your emotions.

Mental self-care —engage in activities that help declutter your mind and reduce your stress levels i.e., meditation, yoga, walks, books, movies, people etc.

Pain

Sometimes you can't take anything from the pain. Sometimes the hurting is too raw and deep, and you can't think of it in any way other than this —you don't want to feel like this ever again. And that is okay. You don't have to look for a lesson in everything. You don't have to find meaning in all your experiences. Sometimes pain is just what it is —*pain*— and there's nothing more to it. I want you to stop listening to those who tell you that your pain has to make sense. That your experiences have to make sense. That somehow all the darkness in your life has to make sense for it to be meaningful. Because it doesn't. Because not every pain has a purpose and not every experience is meant to teach you something. And it is when we fail to find meaning in the hurting that we feel even worse —because how could it hurt this much for nothing *'good'* to come out of it? It's self-destructive to romanticise your scars in this way. To tell yourself *'I'm hurting now but it will all be worth it'*. Because it will be worth it, yes, but not because you are hurting. Not because you are in pain. But because life has to work out. Regardless of how much pain or happiness you experience. Life is worth it *just because it is*. And that is all you need to tell yourself.

Happiness

Maybe what you thought happiness was when you were younger is different to what happiness means to you now. Maybe happiness was being wrapped up in a blanket by your mother's side as you watched TV, or having your father lift you up and twirl you over his head while you screamed at the top of your lungs. Happiness was playing tag with your friends at school and ending the class day with a painting lesson instead of Math. Happiness meant waking up late on Saturday to the waft of buttery pancakes and taking your dog on a walk with the whole family on Sunday. But now happiness is different. Maybe now happiness is your evening bath after a long day at work. Happiness is a weekly phone catch-up with your best friend and a Sunday brunch with your mother. Happiness is binge-watching your favourite Netflix series and reading a novel. Happiness is listening to a Podcast as you dive into your spring cleaning. Happiness is the first hot coffee on Monday as your colleagues fill you in on the gossip of the weekend. Happiness is scrolling through Instagram and sending a hilarious meme to your friend which makes both of you fall into a fit of laughter. Happiness is those crisp cold walks through the park with a scarf wrapped around your neck and a snug coat on, with some good songs to give you company.

Maybe happiness now is not the carefree, childlike joy that you used to feel at the tiniest things when you were younger but the small joys instead. The quiet, tranquil moments that don't need to be expressed or shared with anyone but yourself for them to be instances of pure, relentless happiness.

Happily Ever After

We have been taught our entire lives about a *'happily ever after'*. About the moment everything falls into place after you find *'the one'*. About how easy life is once you have your 'other half', the half that is supposed to make you whole. We have been taught our entire lives about how important it is to find the person you're supposed to journey with that we forget how important our individual journeys are. The ones that continue even after we get into relationships and marriages and families. The journeys that don't somehow get easier after we find the *'right person'* —but in fact become more difficult. We are taught that finding the love of your life is like standing at the peak of a mountain when the reality is so different. Finding the love of your life is like standing at the beginning of that very mountain and starting the climb. It isn't easy and it doesn't get any easier. But still, we have been taught our entire lives that a *'happily ever after'* exists following the declaration of love that we almost start to believe it. And when real life doesn't coincide, when we're faced with hurdles and challenges, and our *'fairy-tale'* is grey with the truth of existence —we understand how false that belief was.

The truth is that life continues even after you find love. With the same struggles. The same internal battles. The same challenges and hurdles and the same trauma. The only thing that falls into place after you find someone to spend the rest of your days with is the faith that even if everything does end up falling apart —you still have someone to go home to. And that is what gives you comfort. That is what eases your heart. That is what changes after you fall in love.

Have you ever thought that perhaps you too are someone else's mistake? A reason for them to break.

A regret. A wound. A hard lesson learned.

Attachment

As much as we tell ourselves that we won't get attached again, that this time things will be different, this time we won't go all in with our hearts, this time we won't let them know our vulnerabilities too soon. This time we won't trust them blindfolded and we won't carry our heart on our sleeve —it's still so difficult to do. And I guess the only way to understand it is to accept the value of love in our lives and how much hope we still have that it is meant for us. Despite getting hurt. Despite having our hearts broken. Despite being shown more than once that love is a verb and not a meaningless word uttered when it is most convenient. Because we are still human. We want to feel cared for and loved and considered. We want to matter. And when someone indicates the slightest possibility of caring for us the way that we wish —we can't help but trust them with all our heart and hope that *this time it will be true.*

Learning

I'm learning that it isn't my job to make people good, and that I don't need to make others realise what they did wrong if they don't see it themselves. I'm learning that kindness isn't always returned with kindness and friendship often with pain, and sometimes you make mistakes that you wish you didn't, and you lose people that you wished would stay —but nothing you do can stop them from going far away from you. I'm learning that healing and hurting often go hand-in-hand, and that the journey is messy, fluctuating and often flooded with enough challenges that make you want to give up. But life is beautiful, experiences lace your path with colour and people —they are the ones that make living worthwhile. I'm learning that I don't need to have everything figured out. I need to focus on my own time-scale rather than focus on what other people are doing with their lives. I need to measure my growth/progress in relation to my previous experiences and struggles instead of other people's success. Everyone's journey is different, and it is only when you appreciate this difference that you can accept everything that your life brings you. I need to focus on me.

I'm learning that I must direct all my energy towards my mind and soul with the hope that it will allow some magic to form. I'm learning that I will continue to learn today, tomorrow and in the days that follow. I'll have experiences that will break me, and bring me joy, and enlighten me in new ways. I'll keep learning until I feel wiser, stronger and more whole. And even then, I'll continue learning —because there is so much in every bend of this world that I can learn, and there's a lot that I need to know before I can say that I know enough. And even when I'll say that I know enough, I'll keep learning. I'll keep going. I'll keep growing along the way.

Imperfect Human

And I have realised that all I really want to do in this life is spend each and every day talking to you. I want to tell you about how my day was and hear about yours. I want to make small talk and drop cute jokes that only the two of us understand because we have a crazy sense of humour. I want to be silly with you and not be one bit embarrassed about the fact that my laughter makes me sound like a snorting pig, because you find it cute and that's enough to make me smile. I want to listen to you speak about your dreams and ambitions and I want you to hear about mine too. I want to spend every day hearing your voice and wondering just how —in this imperfectly beautiful universe— I ended up finding my kind of a perfectly imperfect human.

It is okay to be *'too much'* of everything. Too kind. Too soft. Too loving. Too loud. Too sensitive. Too gentle in a world that forces everyone to turn to stone. Because you are different. You were not made to be just like everyone else. You were made to be too much of everything that they were too little of.

Sometimes it's not about any particular *'goals'* or *'achievements'* but just the need to get through one more day. To fight one more battle with the darkness in your head that tells you to give it all up. Sometimes it's not about creating those high pedestals for yourself that will take years to climb, but instead forming tiny accessible steps that will get you closer to your healing. To a sense of peace and quiet. To happiness. In a world where everyone emphasises the importance of external goals and achievements, where people base the success or failure of their day on how productive they can be —choose to be still instead. Choose to be calm and as slow as you can to ease your journey. Choose to focus on your internal growth before you focus on the external. And choose values such as love, family, and joy to measure the success of your day —because that is what matters the most. Your heart is more important than any goal that you could conquer. Your peace of mind is more important than any materialistic success. Your mental and emotional wellbeing matter so much more than whatever standards society places for you.

Heartbreak

Heartbreaks feel like the end of all your happiness. Sometimes it hurts so much that you almost believe that your heart will explode inside your chest because of the pain. And it kills. It kills to think that the one person whom you thought you would spend the rest of your life with is no longer by your side. It kills to imagine waking up in the morning with the heavy weight of loss at the pit of your heart. It kills when the niggling truth dawns on you —and not for the first time that day— that you can never speak to them again. You can never live out the best parts of your life again. You can never hear their twinkly laughter filled with love for you again. It kills. It does. But it can't destroy you. I promise you. It might feel like it's the end of the world, but read this —it is only the end of the world that you shared with them. It might feel like your life sucks, but read this —this is just a *bad time* in your life. It doesn't mean that your life is bad. It doesn't mean that you won't be happy or find love again, even if it's in your own arms. It doesn't mean that you can't come home to yourself. Because you can and you will. And one day you will be so comfortable with the fact that it didn't work out that when you see them, because life has a funny way of showing you stuff —you will tell them this; '*Loving you almost killed me.* But it didn't. And here I am, still smiling. Still in love with the life that I had before you came. Here I am. Still living. Here I am —still living.'

That is the thing about being a good person. You would never wish for the kind of pain that others inflict on you, and even after you go through it —you won't purposely do the same to them. You just won't. Your heart doesn't work in the same way as theirs. Hurting other people has never been something you were good at, and even if you sometimes cause others pain by letting them down —you end up breaking your own heart because it feels like you let yourself down by hurting them.

People

There will be people in this world who will question you. People who won't be able to see life the way that you do. People who will try to understand your values but still fail because they haven't walked in your shoes. There will be people who won't be able to fall into you the way you wished. People who won't love you back, or hard, or as much as you had hoped. People who will try and try but still won't be able to fit you into the crevices of their life. And you will have to let them go. You will have to tell yourself that it wasn't meant to be. That in a world where souls are made of the same soft golden stardust —yours were different. You will have to admit to your pulsing heart that theirs did not want yours in the same way and you will have to hope —for a morning where it doesn't hurt as much. For a day where the sunshine is able to tumble into all your cracks and make you whole again. For the disappointment that you were not loved as hard to fade, slowly. You will need to hold yourself delicately then, rocking your heart back and forth as you remind yourself that those who don't love you back cannot define you. Those who don't love you back do not determine your worth. Those who don't love you back did not have space for you in their lives —but this doesn't mean that someone else won't.

Tonight is one of those nights where my chest burns with the pain that your heavy absence left long ago.

Some people can never be replaced.

If you were here today you would probably take pride in the worth that this attaches to you. But I take nothing but sorrow from it.

—dear mum

My Heart

I don't know how else to explain to my heart to stop wanting things that aren't good for me. People, situations, and relationships that cause me nothing but pain. I don't know how to make it realise that love is beautiful when it is reciprocated but the same love breaks you in two when it isn't. I don't know how else to tell my heart that you shouldn't chase love or the people you love, and most definitely not when they claim to love you too. But my heart doesn't listen. It keeps chasing you in hope that you will stop running, but if you loved me, you would stay. If you loved me, you would stay —and still my heart doesn't seem to understand things in this way.

Stay Still

You know you are in love when you don't just feel emotions flutter in your chest like flower petals that disappear into the wind —you also feel peace. Inner peace. The kind that you searched for years before finding them. The kind that reminded you of this emptiness within the folds of your heart, but you were never able to place your finger on what it was. You were never able to understand why the days always felt like half a meal that still leaves you hungry. Your heart doesn't just flicker with nerves and excitement when you're in love, it also quells. It quietens. It is no longer agitated or anxious, or scared of the world. You heart feels calm. Relaxed. As though your chest has finally retired from a lifetime of searching for a home before realising that it was the home another heart needed all along.

You see, love isn't just about miracles. Or fantasies. Love isn't about words that flutter in the pages of a romance novel that you can't put down. It is deeper than that. It dwells in the stories that tumble in the author's mind. It is the invisible lines that you trace over your palm, trying to read your own destiny. Love is buried in all your hopes and expectations. It is sharing —vulnerabilities, insecurities, fears, dreams, and lives. Love is understanding and accepting each other's weaknesses. It is more than cute dates and matching outfits. It is persistent. Unwavering. It is real. And you will know it. You will know that you are in love when it is not just the hues of passion that overwhelm you —but also the hues of peace. You will know that you are in love when your heart no longer bounces inside your chest but hushes instead. You will that know you are in love when your heart learns to stay still. You will know it then. When your heart is finally still.

I want you to be happy. I want you to forget all the hurtful memories from a past that made us both who we are —and I want you to move on. I hope that we can be friends one day. Heck, I hope that we can look at each other in the eye without either of us turning our face away because the weight of what has happened is too heavy on both our chests. I want you to know that I wish the best for you. That I want happiness, love, and friendship to fill every crack in your life that I left behind. I want you to be the happiest that you have ever been. I want you to laugh and cry with joy and forget everything that has ever rattled inside your heart. That is what I want. That is what I hope life gives you one day.

Fall Apart

We talk a lot about time healing wounds and things getting easier the further away that horrible event that affected you is. But this doesn't mean that —to begin with— things won't be hard. Because they will. There's an expression that goes something like *'all bad/good things come in threes'* and while this may not be completely true in life —it does help explain those moments in our journey when things are going wrong everywhere. Maybe your love life is damaged or currently healing, but then something really upsetting happens at work too, and along with this —you and your friend fall out. You also had an argument with your mum/dad the other day and now, guess what, you're feeling a little under the weather too. Moments like this in our lives bring us down devastatingly. How could things get any worse than they already are? How could our love life, personal relationships, career/ education, and dreams all mess up at the same time? It sucks. It really does.

But sometimes life needs to fall apart. Everything needs to fall apart. You need to fall apart so you can come together again. We focus so much on the negativity in our lives that we fail to think about why things have gotten this bad? There's clearly something wrong in the current pattern of your life, the dynamics of your relationships and what you are trying to do at work/school/your business that isn't working. None of it is going right because *something is going wrong.* So, rather than focussing too much on feeling bad that things aren't working out for you —start considering all the reasons why those events are happening to begin with and what needs to change for these things to not re-occur. Sometimes things need to get worse before they get better, because the lesson that is in front of you hasn't become evident to you yet. But when it does —things will change for the better. Because they have to.

Drowning

I recently heard this line *'You can't save this relationship by not growing'*, and I can't express how much it resonated with me. It's true, isn't it? Often, we fall in love and in our need to make it work —we stop doing things that our partner might not like. It might not even be on purpose. But still, there are certain changes in your behaviour and appearance that come as a result of your desire to make your partner happy. Sometimes you even stop changing. Stop growing. You push your hobbies away. You no longer meet up with the friends that your partner doesn't like. You think twice about your actions. You always ask yourself, *'Would my partner be okay with this?'*, before buying that outfit, booking that trip, or making a decision about your school or career. Subconsciously, you adjust every part of your life to meet their desires and needs. And slowly, but steadily, you lose yourself. You forget that growth is inevitable. And in your need to please someone else, you are killing the part of you that keeps you going. In your need to save your relationship —you are doing everything that will one day leave you drowning.

The more chances you give someone, the more reason you give them to think that they can do whatever they want and get away with it.

Passers-by

Some people are only meant to cross paths with you —that is all. They are not supposed to stay in your life forever. Some people slip into your life like a rainbow but leave a tornado in their wake —making you doubt love and all the good in your life. Making you question whether they truly had to leave, because if they did —then why did it feel so wrong? Why did it hurt so much? Because if they had to leave then why did they come into your life to begin with? But they had to. Believe me. Some people are passers-by in a journey that is all about your growth, healing, and happiness. These people arrive in the form of daylight and warmth but leave as hard lessons that you stumble over. These people tuck love into the pleats of your heart but leave fragments of themselves behind. These people teach you how to laugh with your eyes closed and they show you —in the truest sense— what it means to let love in. But some people are only a stage in your life. An experience. A temporary fixture. A fleeting moment that won't last forever. And these people, these very soulmates who you would do anything for, teach you that —no matter how much you care for each other— sometimes those you love have to leave, and *you have to let them.*

Time

What if time was nothing but relative to our imagination and we all received the same amount? Is there something you would do different if you knew you only lived until a certain age? Would you try harder to make amends with people, or adopt a skill you didn't have before? It would make it easier, I think, to know that in this time we could do everything we set our heart to because that was all we got. Maybe we would be kinder if we knew that some were closer to the end than others. Maybe we would treat each other better. Be softer. Gentler. Maybe we would value our relationships more than external things and put effort into them instead of a career that doesn't fulfil us. Maybe we would finally tell ourselves to pick up the guitar, or the drum, or the paintbrush and give that dream one shot. Just one. If we knew how little time we had on this earth —would we value it more? Would we stop wasting it on people who don't fulfil us and search for our soulmates instead? Maybe we would travel more and make less excuses.

Maybe we would be riskier with love —loving wholly, loving imperfect, growing souls rather than porcelain-glass ones that look pretty but have nothing to offer. Maybe we would stop saying *'I don't have time'* and try to make more of it. Maybe we would stop saying *'tomorrow'* and start doing today. Maybe we would end each phone call with *'I love you'* and each goodbye with a soul-tight hug. Maybe we would stop acting like we have all the time in the world and start accepting that this time is limited —and we should make the most of it.

Wait for a love that arrives when you least expect it. Love that shows up at your doorstep on a cold wintry evening. Love that takes your hand and presses it against their chest until you can feel their heartbeat. Wait for a love that respects you. Love that doesn't make you second-guess yourself. Love that challenges you to be a better version of yourself. Love that believes in you. Wait for a love that is here for the long run. Love that understands the words *'commitment'* and *'companionship'* and doesn't make excuses for their mistakes. Love that trusts you and tries its best to understand your emotions. Wait for a love that is gentle with your heart. Love that brushes delicate fingers over a hand that has been let go of more than once. Love that knows how much you have gone through to find them. Wait for a love that is there through the difficult days. The messy days. The hard-to-forget days. The days when you are at your worst. And the days that are drunk on laughter and happiness. Wait for a love that holds you through it all, to steady you. To calm your pattering heart. Love that understands how hard it is having a soft soul in a rough, messy world. Love that doesn't try to change you in any way. Wait for a love that stays. A love that stays.

Signs that you are in a toxic friendship:

1. They make you feel bad about yourself.

2. They only talk to you when they need you.

3. They are only around during your most difficult times —not during your happiest moments.

4. They only want to talk about themselves —the conversation is never about you.

5. You don't look forward to your outings with them.

6. You can't trust them with your secrets.

7. They disregard your achievements/happiness.

Have you ever thought that maybe you were the one that got away? The one that changed their meaning of love and relationships forever. The one who turned their life upside down by leaving to such an extent that they were never the same again. Have you ever wondered that perhaps it didn't work out because you were the lesson for them? The essential tool. The thorn of heartache that had to sting them once so it wouldn't sting them again. Because you keep telling yourself that you should have been better. That you should have tried harder. Been stronger. Loved them more. But maybe you did everything that you could, and it still didn't work out because they weren't ready for a heart like yours. And it took you leaving and breaking both your hearts in two for them to finally understand what it means to love someone like you.

Accept Your Pain

Before, I used to scold myself whenever I felt sad. I told myself that it is not okay to feel so low, to let tears spill down my cheeks, to be this vulnerable. You see, we've become so accustomed to putting a mask on in front of the world that sometimes we forget to take it off in front of ourselves too. We forget that being honest with ourselves is the biggest gift we could give our hearts. Listening to our pain, to our trauma. Unveiling our scars. Accepting blemishes. Simmering in the sadness rather than pushing it away, rather that clumping sadness, pain, and trauma under a tight heading, *'Things I don't want to speak about'*, and locking it away in a compartment in our mind. Accept your pain. Embrace it. Let your heart squirm with emotions, both good and bad, and don't brush away the things that make you sad. Listen to them. Understand them. Because they are as much a part of you as everything else is. It's okay to be sad. It's okay to cry. It's okay to feel vulnerable and scared and anxious. Don't be so hard on yourself. You're only human after all. You're only human.

In another world.

In another world, they didn't give up and walk away. In another world, they always held you close. In another world, they loved you more than you loved them. In another world, you grew old together and that was the only life you knew.

In this world, you sit down and wonder how things might have been in another world.

Rest of My Life

You have my entire heart. Every nook, cranny and crevice of this beating bundle is all yours. And I know that I should not give all of me to you. I've been told more than once that I should learn to live without people who have the power to let me go. I know. But I can't help it. I can't help but give you my smiles and tears and all the happy years that I have left ahead. I can't help but imagine a future where I get to live, laugh and grow with you. I can't help but feel like my, *'This is what I've been waiting for'*, moment has become a reality to such an extent that I have to pinch myself sometimes. Because you are that good to me.

And you have my entire heart. You do. Because this heart has been weathered and torn enough in the past to know just what —and how much— it deserves. Because this heart has learned to love itself before it gave others the permission to do so. And in a world where we teach others to be entirely whole and complete —I still choose to give you a tiny piece of me, making me slightly incomplete without that piece of you. And it is okay. It is okay to hug your soul and let you pull mine close and still believe —at the back of my mind— that I have the potential to live without you. Because maybe I can, but *I don't want to.* And it's this choice, this knowing that a world without you is a world in which I will continue to live but *choosing this world* with you anyway. Choosing this moment with you anyway. Choosing you today and tomorrow. And knowing that even though loving you wasn't a choice I made —it happened unexpectedly— keeping you is a choice I will continue to make every single day, for the rest of my life.

For You

It will never be easy. Standing up for yourself. Telling others that you're no longer willing to accept half-hearted promises and a love that is never there. Bunching your hands into fists with a courage that's taken you years to build up. It will never be easy. Admitting to those you love that they did you wrong. Reminding them of the things they said and how their actions never followed through. Pointing out their mistakes and every time they let you down. It will never be easy. Doing what's right for you. Doing something for yourself for once. But you have to do it if you want to be happy in the long run. You have to tell people how you feel, no matter how hard it is. No matter how difficult. No matter what the consequences will be after that. No matter how scared you are. You have to tell people how you feel. Because you have to do it for you.

Affirmations

As someone who spent her entire life trying to please others, I'm not telling you to stop straight away. But what I am saying is this —learn to accept how destructive it is to seek validation from others. It becomes so toxic to a point where you need to be complimented or appreciated or told *'I value you'* in order for your existence to make sense. I have done this my entire life where I've looked to people around me to tell me that I'm doing well. To affirm my dreams and goals. To confirm that I've come *'a long way'* for me to believe it too. And this led to me losing so many people as I grew up because I decided to stop seeking that external validation. Because suddenly our relationship didn't make sense. My no longer needing them for affirmation meant they had to re-assess their role in my life to someone who was equal to me —and they couldn't accept that. People whom you look at for constant validation start to believe that they are better than you. That you need them. That if they weren't around, you wouldn't be able to function normally. And when you take that power away from them —neither of your roles make sense anymore. So, before it's too late and you lose some of the most important relationships of your life, slowly start to validate yourself and create a new role for others. One that takes your worth *without their affirmation* into consideration.

Love is Love

Love can't be defined. I can tell you a list of things that remind me of love; actions that describe moments of love, and instances when your pressing emotions have drawn love in so deep —but I can't define love for you. Love isn't a simple word that we can put in the dictionary and understand with concepts that are all man-made. Because love is beyond that. It's not a fleeting feeling or a mere action but a pull —of hearts, words, emotions, thoughts, minds and so much more. I can tell you that love is kisses tossed between grand gestures in the rain. I can tell you that love is their hand resting on your leg during long drives across the countryside. Love is sneaking side glances in a room clustered with drinks, people, and music. Love is losing track of time no matter where you go —whether it's mountains, dinners or the shop down the street; the moment they leave, sadness can't help but tug at your heartstrings. I can tell you that love is laughing uncontrollably and pulling each other's leg. Love is supporting, encouraging, and caring without any expectations. Love is sipping from the same cup and threading your fingers through theirs when you sit across them at lunch. Love is looking at them through eyes drenched with emotion so deep it could drown you both. Love is smiling through those very eyes because you can't help it. I can tell you that love is cuddling under the stars and telling jokes that no one else understands. Love is bickering and going full PDA in a matter of minutes.

I can tell you that love is sharing stories, vulnerabilities, and secrets —but no matter what I say, it still won't be enough. Because love is every single one of those things and so much more. It is the actions that push you and the emotions that pull. It is your peace of mind, sure, but it is also the tremble of nerves that course through you. I could write a whole list of things about love, and it still wouldn't be enough. Because love is a reflection of all those moments and others that we can't put in words. Feelings that we're unable to comprehend. Instances in our life where we sense a flash of emotion, or a flutter of pain and we can't pinpoint exactly what it is. That is still love. That is still a case of a sentiment that can't be defined. It can't be expressed. So, yes —I can write in words what examples of love are, but I can't describe the intricate feelings to you. I can't tell you exactly what that incredible tremble in my heart is when I realise *'I love this person'*, and maybe you can't too.

Because at the end of it, there is no other way to describe it than to accept that *love is just love.*

It is difficult right now. It hurts, I know it hurts but trust me —this will fade. The hurt will disappear, and the memories will fade. Just hold on. Just keep going. Have faith. Believe in the bigger plan and know that even if you're not there yet, you will get there eventually.

Battles

Some of the hardest battles in our lives, the ones that push invaluable teachings on us and allow us to grow, need to be fought alone. No one else can save you other than you yourself. No one else heal you. No one else can fight your wars or quell the monsters in your head. No one else can give you the missing pieces of your heart back to make you whole again. No one else can fix you. It is up to you to focus on your healing. It is up to you to face your problems. It is up to you to fight back, to push the darkness away, to let the light shine through, and to welcome happiness and to be genuinely happy. But this doesn't mean that you need to walk alone. This doesn't mean that you must take your healing journey by yourself. This doesn't mean that you need to push away others when they want to help you or love you, and when they want to be your friend. When they want to support you. No. Embrace friendships. Welcome love into your life again —all kinds of love. Dance, laugh and cry with joy along with those who make you smile. Let them help you. Let them guide you. Let them be there for you while you work on yourself. Let those who love you and care about you put the time and effort they want into you. Don't push people away. Don't push happiness away. Don't push love away.

Yes, this journey is yours to take, and your problems can't be fixed by anyone but you. But this doesn't mean that *your people* can't bring you peace or make it easier for you to fight your battles. It doesn't mean that others can't give you courage or support. It doesn't mean that the compassion of others doesn't have the power to calm the ache in your chest. Because it does. *It can.* People can help you on your healing journey.

They just can't take your journey for you —that's all. So, go ahead and do what you need to do alone. But remember, you don't have to be alone in your life —without the love and care and friendship of others— to do it. Some of the best healing journeys are the ones that you take together.

Believe me. You do.

'Self-love'

These days people use the banner *'self-love'* as a justification for hurting others. Because if you're putting yourself first —even if it's at the cost of someone else's happiness— then it's okay, right? *Wrong.* Yes, self-love is important. Prioritising your needs and what you deserve is vital, but this should not come at the cost of someone else's happiness. Especially if you can help it. Especially if you could have prevented that person from breaking their heart or falling apart in more than one way. Because self-love doesn't justify being selfish or mean. Self-love doesn't justify doing things that would lead others astray. Self-love doesn't justify bringing negative energy into someone else's life. It just doesn't. Because you have responsibility to other people and downright disregarding that by doing things for your own gain —or leaving them without answers, or a valid explanation for why you treated them in that way— isn't you practicing self-love. Doing what you want rather than what you have a responsibility to do isn't you practicing self-love. Because you are using *'I need to prioritise myself'* as an excuse to hurt other people. You are using it as an excuse to do what you please without worrying about how much hurt it will cause. Especially if you know what the consequences of your actions will be. And if you can help it —don't hurt others for your own personal gain. Because self-love is so much more than that. Self-love is so much more than trying to use it as an excuse to be selfish.

And look at this, that person —without whom you thought you couldn't live a moment— doesn't cross even the barest corners of your mind anymore.

It's funny how time manages to paint over even the

deepest wounds.

'Right Person'

The truth is that the right person is just a figment of our imagination. This idea that one day we will come across someone who will be *'so perfect'* has been pushed into our mind through social media, movies, and books to such an extent that anyone who appears less than that is instantly rejected by our mind. And —don't get me wrong— they're right to an extent about how magical love and relationships can be, but most of the time they are wrong. Because others don't tell you that it's fine to fall in love with someone who's still growing and working on themselves. Others don't tell you that you're not going to appreciate *all* the personality traits of the person that you fall in love with. In fact, sometimes you will find them annoying and stubborn —but you will love them anyway. Even though a deep frown appears on their face on days when they are moody, the skin between their eyebrows bundling up like a duvet. Even though their voice is louder than yours when you're having disagreements, causing others to turn their head in disdain. Even though they always refuse to listen to you before making a mistake and you have to swallow down the urge to say *'I told you so'* —but most of the time you say it anyway. Even though their words have made you cry more than once. You will still love them.

And it's not because you will love their imperfections because it's wrong to think you can love *everything* about someone else. It's because *you will love them.* And the other things —the stubbornness, the annoying habits, the moods, the impatience and so on— it will be stuff you accept *because* you love them. Not because they are perfect. Not because they are *'right'* in every sense of the word. But because they *feel* right. And this is different to finding someone who is so perfect for you that nothing can go wrong. Because this is about taking chances. This is about knowing that things could go wrong and your perception on lots of stuff is different —but still accepting them and loving them anyway. This is about choosing to work on something that's not faultless but seeing the potential in it. This is about knowing —for sure— that movies and books and songs have it all wrong because there is no *'right person'*. There is just a person —your person. The person you want to spend the rest of your life with. The person who makes you laugh and smile but annoys the hell out of you, but you love them anyway. The person whose bad morning-breath and dirty laundry over the floor get on your nerves more than once —but you accept it. You compromise. You adjust and you make it work because you love them.

And the *'right person'* can be wrong, on many occasions, more than once and in ways you never expected. But you choose to forgive them for what matters. You choose to work on it. You both make mistakes, learn and grow until you can be certain that this relationship is what you want and what you deserve.

The problem isn't feeling negative emotions, the problem is being unable to express these emotions to others. How do I tell you what's going on in my mind when I don't understand it myself? There are good days, days when the smile on my lips reaches my eyes and I don't feel sadness touch a single part of me. But those days are rare, and a lot of the time —darkness takes a hold of my soul in a way I can't comprehend. I don't know why I feel like this. I wish that I could explain it, but I can't. And it's eating me up. The problem is the inability to express the emotional turmoil inside me, the inability to look at someone and say, *'I need help, but I don't know what sort'*. Because I used to think that help implies desperation, but it doesn't, and even though I'm not desperate to be saved —it would be nice to have positive thoughts once in a while. It would be nice to sit down with my family and friends and *not feel empty.* The problem isn't what is going on inside me, because I know that I'm not the only one who feels this way —so, I know that I'm not going insane. The problem is being unable to share this emotion with others because of the hot fear at the back of my mind that tells me —despite having similar feelings— they still won't understand. The problem is being afraid that I'll get misjudged or labelled as something that I'm not. The problem is feeling alone in a room crowded with people that I love.

The problem is wanting someone to listen to me, but not knowing exactly what I have to do to be heard.

—mental health: a taboo

Work on Yourself

When you say that you're *'working on'* yourself, what do you mean? Because if it's continuing the same routine that you have had for years in hope that you will find what you're looking for within —then you're doing it all wrong. If you're working on yourself then *truly work on yourself.* Start a journal. Take long baths. Sleep for at least 8 hours a night. Begin saying *'no'* to things that you don't want to do and make more time for things that you do. And if you don't know what you want —then do a brainstorm. Start cooking fresh meals and make effort to grab a coffee with your friend, and call your mother to have that difficult conversation that you've been putting off for so long. Do some trauma work. Focus on ways to ease your anxiety. Go on walks. Listen to health and positivity podcasts. Watch comedy skits. Read self-help books and stories that inspire you. Listen to uplifting music. Watch great movies.

The point is —be in motion. It's not enough to continue the same routine that you've had for the last few years. Because working on yourself requires effort. It requires change. It requires you to step out of your comfort zone and try new things. It requires you to talk about the difficult stuff, the scary stuff, the painful and heart-breaking stuff. Because if you want to grow then you truly need to work on yourself and for that —you need to do something, anything, rather than nothing at all.

Relationships

Trusting people, caring for them and loving them means giving them the right to hurt you. It's simple. You can't tell yourself that other people aren't capable of causing you pain. That they are not capable of doing something wrong. No one is perfect and those you love are capable of making mistakes that can shake your small world in more than one way. There may come a time when they put themselves first— and rightly so— but it might be at odds with what you want. It might cause you pain. Those you love can let you down and forget the promises that they made. But this doesn't mean that your friendship or relationship is over. It just means that things have gone wrong, and you might need to fix them. You might need to work on it a little harder. You might need to re-evaluate your relationship. Mistakes don't necessarily mean that it's the end —but yes, some do. And it's up to you to decide whether it's worth saving or not. But don't live with the belief that those you love cannot/will not hurt you. They will. Maybe more than once. And it's on you to decide whether it's a mistake worth forgiving or whether it's time to close old chapters and move on.

People aren't meant to stay in your life forever. Even if *'forever'* was a thing and relationships lasted a lifetime, certain relationships have to fall apart in order for us to grow. To learn. To come to terms with what we want and what we deserve, and how sometimes those two things might align but sometimes they won't, and we have to accept that. We have to embrace it in order to be truly happy in our life. Not everyone is going to be by our side and sometimes —even after people leave— we will carry a piece of them in our hearts for a long time before we can truly move on. And that's just how life is. It is a cycle of loving, learning, and healing —and in the process, shedding parts of who you used to be and growing into who you are supposed to become.

Your heart is the only home I want for myself. Your arms are all that can keep me warm on a cold wintry evening. You are everything that I could have wanted for myself, and so, so much more.

4 tips on how to deal with heartbreak:

1. Get out of denial —accept that it's over.

2. Let yourself feel the emotions —it's important to grieve what you have lost.

3. Don't let your feelings overwhelm you —make sure that you don't *become* your feelings.

4. Get closure —this doesn't need to take place with the other person. You can give yourself closure; have that difficult conversation and answer your own questions.

Wait For Them

I was meant to learn about life this way. I had to stumble and fall and crack my heart in two before finding someone who showed me what home feels like. Before finding someone who didn't just teach me about friendship, respect and compassion but also love —*in its truest sense*. I thought that I knew what love was. I thought that the pain I had experienced on the hands of others was *my whole experience of love combined.* I thought that my yesteryears had painted a picture of love so clear that nothing else after that would change my mind. But I was so wrong. And I'm glad that I learned about love this way. I had to walk through hard thorns to meet the one person who would change my life forever. I had to bend backwards to fit into other people's stories before I stumbled across someone who showed me what it's like to embrace myself entirely. Someone who taught me what it's like to be comfortable in my skin, and to stand up, head held high, shoulders spread wide as I refused to bend for others any longer. Someone who not only changed my definition of love forever but showed me that nothing before them could ever come close to what love truly was.

I'm glad that I lost myself in a life-long journey of healing to finally find myself on my own accord with someone who wants to walk alongside me. With someone who taught me that love is kind, soft and easy on you. That love is gentle. And warm. And consistent. That love isn't having to fight for what you deserve and settling for less. Love isn't harsh or selfish or mean to you. I'm so glad that I finally met someone who showed me that nothing before them was real and nothing after could compare to the kind of love that they have made my heart feel.

Broken

It kills to know that I have to leave you behind. And not just you but every ounce of memory and love that we shared. It kills to think that I won't be able to pick up the phone whenever I want to ring you. To check up on you. To tell you how my day has been and how difficult life can be sometimes. I can't imagine not ranting to you. Or crying. Or complaining that you don't give me as much time as your friends. Or just talking. About anything and everything. It's like my heart has been torn in two and you have taken the bigger piece. The piece that always kept me afloat. But that's just how love is —isn't it? Sometimes love is the wind that sets you free and sometimes it is a cage of memories so strong that even thinking about leaving is difficult. Even imagining another day without them by your side is as hard as breathing with no air. Even telling yourself that it is time to go hurts like a scraping wound. Even turning away to look at a future without them rips your heart in two. And you just have to accept it, because there's nothing else you can do.

I live in a generation filled with people who believe that love is skin deep, with people who don't know how to

love someone's *soul*.

Trust

Loving you has been easy —believe me. It is learning to trust someone new that has been hard. Having a heart that has been trampled all over in the past does that to a person. Where, even if someone magical comes along, with a soul that gives more than it takes —you still can't help but fear. You still can't help but overthink. You can't help the niggling voice at the back of your mind that repeats, *'This is too good to be true'*. But it is true. It is real. You are real, in every sense, in every way. You're real when you pick me up after a long day at work. You're real when you buy me roses and chocolate to celebrate nothing other than us. You're real when you take my hand and kiss it out of the blue. You're real when you make tea and bring the snacks on our adventures. You're real when you call me each morning and ask me, *'So, when are we meeting today?'*, because you miss me so much. You're real when you make spontaneous plans for picnics and cute dates. You're real when you tell me that you love me and mean it with all your heart.

But trusting new people has never been easy for me. Learning with experience that most people are only here for a good time and the moment they notice your imperfections —they jet out the back door before you can ask them why. And because of this, no matter how real you are, no matter how incredible you are —I find it difficult to pour my entire trust into you. Even though I know that you would use all your energy in ensuring that you don't break it. Even though you would happily spend the rest of your life convincing me that I made the right choice —not through persistent actions or words *but just by being you.* Even though placing my trust in your hand is no different to placing my heart in it —I still struggle. And maybe I will continue to struggle until I accept with every particle that you won't break my trust. But until that day —the one where I place you on a pedestal higher than any other person in my life —I will keep believing in how real you are. In how honest and true you are. In how gentle you are. And I will keep letting you love me. Through our tumbling days. Through the pulsing nights. Through each high and low that life brings us. I will keep letting you love me.

I hope that you're able to find all the happiness that you are looking for in others inside your own magical, starry heart. I hope that you find the strength to flood your heart with a love so deep that you never pine for someone else again. And you accept that honest, raw love doesn't come with conditions. It doesn't come with false promises and shallow actions. It doesn't come with people who always take you for granted and never treat you right. I hope that you're able to protect yourself from those who never valued you, from those who never appreciated your gentleness, your kindness and your soft, warm soul. I hope that you find something true within yourself. A light so bright it can't be ignored. I hope that you find a purpose. A drive. A will to keep your head high —despite it all.

Boundaries

Setting boundaries should not be hard. But it feels like the most difficult thing to do when you're not used to laying out your expectations for others. It's so difficult to look at those that you care about and express to them —for the first time in a long time— that you don't appreciate being treated a certain way, or that you don't want to visit a particular topic, or that you believe it's not right to go somewhere because it's crippling for your mental/emotional health. Because you feel guilty. You feel bad for saying *'no'* because you've never said it before. You have never told others what is or isn't okay with you. You've never carved a line which they should not cross. So, the moment that you do —they can't grasp what's going on.

Because suddenly they feel like they've been set boundaries when really, you're the one *who set them for yourself.* Because suddenly your boundaries become a line that they can't cross, and others don't like being told what they can and can't do. But listen to this —if they love you, they will respect your boundaries. If they care about you, they will welcome the lines you draw because they will recognise that you haven't placed them there for no reason. They will understand that it took immense courage for you to express —for once– – about the stuff that triggers you. And even if they can't understand it —*they will try.* They will try to be gentler and more considerate. Because you set those boundaries. Because you told them what you can and can't accept in the nicest way possible. And the least they can do is respect that. The least they can do is give you the space that you deserve.

Maybe right now is not the time for love or relationships —but the time to find yourself. Maybe you spent so many years trying to secure trickles of meaning in other people's words that it's time for you to turn to yourself for love. For value. Maybe the time you spent pouring your softness into others was supposed to be spent with yourself, in your own company, turning to your own arms for the comfort and love that you sought for in others. And that's why this is not the time for relationships or love. That's why this is the time for you to turn to yourself to do the necessary soul-searching. To heal. To learn and grow and get closer to becoming the person you need yourself to be.

I know that it's scary to let someone else in. To show another person your vulnerabilities. To give them permission to peek inside your heart and see all your scars. To welcome them in, knowing that they will be able to see your previous trauma. It is so damn scary knowing that maybe they won't stay forever but if they leave —they will take a piece of everything that you have given with them. But to love truly, and honestly, is to go all in. If you want to make it work, you have to trust the fall —the one that doesn't guarantee you hurting but will definitely give you the wings that you need to fly. If you want to make relationships work, you need to put everything in. You need to give it your 110% and feel it with all your heart and believe that it will work. It has to. And if it doesn't, if —after everything you both have experienced— you decide to part ways, at least you can say that you tried. That you gave it your best shot. That you weren't afraid of falling. Of getting your heart broken. Instead, you were excited about the journey. The one that taught you so much more than just about love. The journey that gave you a glimpse inside another's heart and showed you just how raw and vulnerable they are too. The journey that allowed you to see that you may have scars —but they don't make you any less worthy of loving.

Destiny

When I was younger, I didn't understand why my life was so difficult. I would see other children my age with a normal-looking life, and I wondered why I had it so hard. Why did God decide that someone as young as me was meant to go through all those trials and tribulations? I was too young to understand what any of it meant or what the purpose of those battles was then. But now I understand. You see, I spent most of my life comparing myself to people who *'appeared'* to have a better life than me, but I never looked the other way. I never comprehended that perhaps my life was difficult —but so was everyone else's. In fact, some people had it even worse than me. And this was not to make myself feel better about my life —*but to make me see sense.* It was to make me realise that every single one of us must go through our share of challenges and struggles, the same way that every clay pot is meant to be moulded and shaped. But these struggles will vary —just like those clay pots will be moulded differently— because their end goal is not the same. What they are supposed to be differs, and that is why some clay pots are pushed to bend themselves whereas others are pulled and stretched.

In the same way, our destiny is not the same. Who we're supposed to be isn't the same. And while some of us have to bend more, others are stretched more and each of us has our boundaries tested so we can become the people that we're meant to be. So, even though some people *'appear'* to have a life better than ours, they also have their own challenges and battles to face —ones that will stretch them beyond their control and place them exactly where they are supposed to be.

I guess I never understood why you said that my love wasn't right for you, because the last time I checked —there wasn't a right or wrong way of loving someone.

Walk Away Again

And when you fall in love again —remember how it felt to love the wrong person. Remember the tears, anguish, and hurt. Remember constantly making excuses for them and telling yourself that they *'still love me'* even though they didn't show up, even though they treated you with actions that spoke louder than words, even though they let you down more than once. When you fall in love again —remember how you curled inwards, losing yourself, forgetting to smile or take care of yourself. Remember that loving someone so wrong for you —so deeply— brings with it nothing good. And if this time round, when you fall in love again, they have the same scent of forgotten promises and half-hearted *I love you's* —remember how hard you fell last time. Remember how much it hurt to let them go. Remember the bitter aftertaste of regret that followed because you didn't leave them sooner. Remember it enough so you can remind yourself to walk away again.

This journey is yours to take and you have to believe that everything in your life is working in your favour. So, take chances. Step out of your comfort zone. Make new friends and dive into new experiences that you would never have had before today. Stand up for your heart when you know that you should. But don't let those you love to be treated any less either. Put your needs first and put their love right next to it, and take this time to go on the biggest adventure that life could offer you. Live. Breathe. And love. Every day is a new day.

Sooner

Some of the hardest moments of my life have prepared me for the kind of courage I would never have had if life had been easy. This doesn't mean that I want to experience pain or that getting hurt doesn't bother me —but it means that rather than seeing pain as a hindrance to my growth; I see it as a necessary tool. Pain has taught me things that happiness never could. Pain has allowed me to understand how fleeting everything is, how temporary the *'good times'* can be and just how unpredictable life is. Pain allowed me to understand the importance of learning about myself and what would be good for me. Pain pushed me to change, grow and shape myself in new ways. And I'm not saying that pain is something we should all experience in order to reach those places, but what I am saying is this —hurting will not stop you from being your happiest self one day. In fact, it might even give you the strength that you need to get there sooner.

Loving You

Loving you hasn't been terrifying or scary like I thought it would be. It's weird because after everything my heart has gone through —I thought I would be jumping into an ocean without knowing how to swim when I fell for you. But you showed me that love doesn't have to make you afraid. You showed me how soft others can be to your heart when they know how to take care of it. You showed me that words can be actions and some actions change your life for the better without you having any idea that it was going to happen. Because loving you was never part of the plan —but it happened anyway. And it has been one heck of an adventure. I've realised now how beautiful love can be when it's healthy and good for you. I've realised now how comforting love is, especially when you don't expect it. I've realised now that love isn't about crazy expectations or butterflies in my stomach but a lifetime of adventures. You showed me that love doesn't have to break your heart. Love doesn't have to hurt you. Love doesn't have to be rough or messy. Love doesn't have to be hard. Because you showed me how beautiful love is when you're with someone who treats you right.

Friendship

How many of you have had friends who promised you that they would always be there for you, but were never there during your moments of happiness? Friends who turned up at your doorstep the moment you had a bad experience but would never cheer you on when you were going through something good. Friends who made toxic comments such as *'I'm so jealous!'* when you told them about a promotion, a new love interest or a holiday. Friends who would ask you passive aggressive questions about stuff that you'd never considered, but this would lead you to questioning those very things yourself? Friends who made honey-coated snide comments which you brushed off as nothing other than *'appreciation'* but really it was their jealousy and unhappiness that they would constantly reflect on you. Friends who gave you their shoulder to cry on every single time but never so much as gave you a *'Congratulations, I'm so happy for you'* and meant it. Truly meant it.

These people just leeched off on your sadness. They got the upper-hand when things weren't going right in your life because on those occasions you relied on them —for advice, for support and encouragement. You turning to them every time you got in a hot mess or you relying on them for advice on all the important matters in your life gave them power. And even if it wasn't on purpose —most of the time it isn't— when that power was taken away, so was their love for you. And no matter how much they would try to be happy in your happiness, no matter how much they would tell themselves —and you— that they want the best for you; they weren't able to achieve this. Because you no longer sought external validation from them. You no longer relied on them in the way you had before. You were no longer an empty jar that they could fill with their validating comments. And that is when you parted ways. That is when you realised that the friendship you cherished was over.

Fleeting Memories

People leave, and that's the truth. Not everyone is going to play a part in your life forever and sometimes the shortest journeys with others tend to have the biggest impact on you. Some friendships don't last forever, and even if they seem to —they definitely don't withstand the hammer of time that shapes them into something different. Lovers become ex-lovers and families break apart and during this time you tell yourself that you've forgotten them, but you can't pretend like forgetting is as easy as wiping a blackboard clean —because it's not. Some people will leave their imprint on your heart forever and even though you will move on, even though you won't spend another day thinking about them, or longing for those honeyed memories of a time when you were the happiest, or pining for someone who had to break you down for you to realise your worth —you will still take them forward with you, as an idea, as a feeling or as a fleeting memory that will live in a tight corner of your mind. Because it will be a reminder of everything that you had to go through to become who you are today. And that is powerful.

I either give too much or too little. Love too much or not at all. Hurt too much or feel numb to the core.

This all-or-nothing approach to life will either drain my soul or destroy the last bit of sanity I have left. And I don't know which one I want to hold onto more.

The year 2020 has been one of resilience. Of strength. It has taken so much out of us that it is hard to believe that we haven't crossed an entire lifetime in 12 months. And while it's been an incredibly difficult year that tested us in numerable ways, it has also been a time of immense healing. Of courage. Of human connection. Of forming new relationships and taking some of the most unique journeys of our lives which we wouldn't have had this year not happened. And even though there are so many *what ifs* that I hold in my heart for this year —there are also so many memorable experiences. I hold so much gratefulness for what this year taught me. I hold love for all my dear ones, and I hold compassion for everyone who stepped in and showed humanity. And I hold hope —so much of it. Hope for a better tomorrow. Hope for all the darkness to slowly fade and hope that the new year brings with it enough light to keep us all going. Enough light to allow us all to continue fighting our personal battles. Enough light to show us that no matter how difficult life gets —we will get through it somehow. We always do.

—an ode to the year 2020

Healing

Maybe we are healing our entire lives. From our firsts, and from the lasts. From our losses. From the broken friendships and broken hearts. From the childhood experiences that we wish we could forget. Maybe we never truly reach an *'end point'* in our healing because we weren't meant to. Because healing is not an upward curve but a line that staggers through the tunnels of love, loss, and growth —which we have to try our best *to sail through, and not out of.* Maybe our healing isn't about reaching somewhere but about moving —forward, onwards, away from the trauma and the cutting wounds of our past. Maybe it was never about forgetting our difficult days and lonesome nights but about understanding how to take them forward with us. It wasn't about *pushing away* the pain but allowing it to *live with us* —by becoming a lesson for growth. Maybe we spend our entire lives running away from the things that we were meant to hold on to, the things that —instead of being a weight on our back— were meant to be the tools that we would keep in our rucksack and take out at every bend of the adventure that we call life.

Remember

How can you think that you are weak? Remember the first time that you broke your heart, failed at something, or had a fight with your friend and thought to yourself —*this is it; I will never be okay.* But time passed and you wrapped yourself with the thread of strength as you forgave, accepted new things, and learned to love again. Remember the number of times you had to pick up after other people, moments when you were the one who had to clean up the mess, when you had to make amends and be the bigger person. Remember the first time you felt pain —deep, restless pain in your ribs. The kind of pain that you could physically feel in your heart. Remember when you believed that you can never come through from this pain, when you hugged a corner of your room and turned off all the lights until they resembled the darkness within you. Remember the months that followed — waking up each morning with the weight of heartache in your chest, and how hard it was to plant a smile on your face when your insides were clenching. But remember how you pulled through, how you learned to not only smile but laugh again, how you adventured, experienced, and waltzed through so many new things that made you, *you.* Things that changed you so much that the old you would have never recognised the person you became.

Remember how you once believed that the ache you felt would never go away, and then remember how it did —how, one morning you woke up to sunlight dripping on your face and you felt the warmth melt your heart into whole again. So, how can you think that you're weak when you have gone through so much and come out stronger? Because remember when you told yourself that you would never be okay again, remember when you believed that your life was over. But then you went ahead and built a new life for yourself anyway. You went ahead and beat all the odds. Remember when you started to believe in yourself. Remember when you started to live.

A Message from The Author

I compiled this book at a time in my life when I experienced loss. Deep loss. A close family member of mine passed away and this left me shaken in more than one way. I had never witnessed someone's death before. I was so young when my mother passed away that I can barely remember her face, let alone how it would have felt to lose her. Never having my mother by my side was the only life I had ever known. But he existed. He was real. He held my hand during the toughest moments of my life. He took care of me. He loved me. He protected me like his own child, and suddenly —out of nowhere— he was gone. So, this loss felt even more personal. It came as a shock, and it hurt like hell. And worst of all —it took so much with it. The life I lived before this loss was different to the life I lived after. I became more recluse. Lost. I would find my mind wandering in odd places without realising it, and when I would notice that I was staring at a random person, or driving without actually looking at the road ahead —I would give myself the metaphorical nudge on the head, as if to say,

'Ruby, what's wrong with you?'

The loss that followed *this loss* was perhaps worse. I don't know how else to explain it other than —some relationships in my life were over and there was no way that things would be the same again. And I think that is the part that hit me the most. The unpredictability of life. The fact that you don't know when your conversation with someone will be the last. When your tight hug will be the last because the one after that will be tinged with awkwardness and unclarity as to where you stand in each other's lives. When your shared smiles and moments of being there for each other will dissolve into a time you wish you could go back to. And this makes me wonder —if we could foresee the end date of our relationships (with friends, family, couples etc.) would we pay more attention to them? Would we hug them a little tighter? Would we hold their hand as though it would imprint it on our palm so the next time we looked down; we could almost feel what it was like to touch them? Would we care more? Show up more? Love them a lot more?

Because now, all I have is a lifetime of memories with those who left before I could turn to them and say *'Remember when...'*

About the Author

Ruby Dhal is a British Afghan-Sikh bestselling author, content creator and speaker. Ruby has written five books of poetry, prose and bite-size self-help on various topics such as heartbreak, healing, grief, self-love, loss, mental health and moving on. She has a social media following of over half a million and her books have made a home for themselves in every corner of the world. Ruby's words have been shared and appreciated by countless celebrities, mentors, and self-help coaches, as well as other bestselling authors.

After losing her mother at the age of 4, Ruby turned to books as a form of escapism and soon developed a love for reading stories and writing. Her only dream was to be a novelist one day. Ruby completed a Philosophy degree from UCL and an MA in Philosophy from King's College London before joining a team in Children's Services. Through her own childhood experiences —as well as through her new role in CS— Ruby learned about the negative impact of domestic abuse, poor choices and minimal opportunities for young people stuck in the same cycle as their parents. Ruby's only goal was to encourage young people to make different choices to their parents and to find hope in all the opportunities that were before them. Ruby uses her words, her social media platform, and workshops in schools to shed light on the importance of stepping out of the darkness that young people find themselves in, and to let their experiences build them rather than break them.

Ruby wants to continue writing non-fiction but also expand into novels which depict the lives of underprivileged POC in a powerful manner to stimulate positive change and create a new dialogue of their lived experiences.

Ruby's purpose is to make an impact through the power of words and storytelling. She wants her writing to make a positive change in the world and inspire readers in a way that allows them to flourish. Ruby believes that everyone has a purpose and once you find your purpose, you should follow it with all your heart. She has found her purpose in writing to make a difference. It is for this reason that Ruby is eager to write, share content and continue changing the world one word at a time. Presently, Ruby is working on the first draft of her debut novel which she will find a home for in the fall of 2021. Ruby believes in writing books that tell honest and uplifting stories that shed light on BAME characters' lives —because theirs are the least voiced. Therefore, all of Ruby's stories are raw, real, and reflective of the lives of innumerable POC.

Ruby also has a travelling/lifestyle page on Instagram (@r.dhalblogger) which she created to share her passion for travelling, food and books along with nuggets of wisdom to a new genre of viewers. You can find Ruby on Instagram (@r.dhalwriter), Facebook (@r.dhalwriter), Tiktok (@r.dhalwriter), YouTube (Ruby Dhal) and Twitter (@rdhalwriter).

Lastly, Ruby holds healing sessions via zoom (video/audio), and email, as well as mentoring sessions and workshops. You can find all the relevant information about the work Ruby does, as well as her blog, on www.rubydhal.com.